X Doesn't Mark the Spot

Tales of Pirate Gold, Buried Treasure, and Lost Riches

ED BUTTS

Tundra Books

Published in Canada by Tundra Books,
75 Sherbourne Street, Toronto, Ontario M5A 2P9

Published in the United States by Tundra Books of Northern New York,
P.O. Box 1030, Plattsburgh, New York 12901

Library of Congress Control Number: 2007943127

Library and Archives Canada Cataloguing in Publication

Butts, Edward, 1951-
      X doesn't mark the spot : tales of pirate gold, buried treasure, and lost riches /
Ed Butts.

Includes bibliographical references.
ISBN 978-0-88776-808-8

1. Treasure troves – Canada – Juvenile literature.   I. Title.

G525.B88 2008   j971   C2007-907588-6

We acknowledge the financial support of the Government of Canada through the Book Publishing Industry Development Program (BPIDP) and that of the Government of Ontario through the Ontario Media Development Corporation's Ontario Book Initiative. We further acknowledge the support of the Canada Council for the Arts and the Ontario Arts Council for our publishing program.

ONTARIO ARTS COUNCIL
CONSEIL DES ARTS DE L'ONTARIO

Design: Jennifer Lum
Typeset in Bembo

Printed and bound in Canada

This book is printed on acid-free paper that is 30% post-consumer waste recycled paper.

1 2 3 4 5 6   13 12 11 10 09 08

For Melanie and Austin,
my two greatest treasures

TABLE OF CONTENTS

INTRODUCTION

Who has not dreamed of becoming fabulously rich overnight; of suddenly having enough money to buy anything or travel anywhere? Many people today buy lottery tickets, with the hope that when the draw is made, they will be big winners. It was with the same high hopes that people of bygone days (and even some today) searched for treasure.

Canadian lore is full of treasure stories – tales of buried pirate booty, of hidden outlaw loot, of wrecked ships loaded with gold and silver, and of "lost" gold mines. Some of the stories, of course, are just tall tales based on little or no factual evidence. Many a dreamer has wasted money, energy, and perhaps even a lifetime chasing after a pot of gold that never existed.

But some hidden treasures *are* real, even if many of the stories about them are exaggerated. Ships laden with gold and silver did sink in Canadian waters. Canada's East Coast was once infested with pirates. Many of these sea-bandits are believed to have buried their plunder, and often ships' captains would go ashore to bury money and other valuables to keep them from falling into pirate hands. And just as often those hidden treasures were never recovered.

In times of war and social unrest, people would hide money, silver plate, jewelry and other cherished items so they wouldn't be stolen by soldiers or looters. They might conceal them behind the bricks of a fireplace, or bury them in a field. Again, circumstances did not always allow people to recover their property.

Although Canada is rich in mineral resources, including gold and silver, the deposits are often in remote, hard-to-reach places. There are numerous stories about prospectors who hit "pay dirt," and then fell victim to some misfortune without telling anyone the location of their bonanza.

As for those who hunted these lost treasures, some were driven by greed. Others were adventurers, drawn as much by the challenge and mystery as they were by the prospect of great wealth. A few got lucky. Most did not.

Many treasure stories are shrouded in superstition. They came down to us from an age in which people firmly believed in ghosts and unseen demonic powers. People believed that pirates were in league with the devil and used black magic to protect their hidden plunder. If a treasure hunter came home empty-handed, he was just as likely to blame his failure on supernatural intervention as to admit that the secret hoard did not exist and he'd been on a fool's errand.

Here then, are eleven tales – both factual and fanciful – of Canadian treasure. They come to us from the East Coast, from Central Canada, and from the West. They are stories of adventure, of shattered hopes, and – occasionally – of dreams come true.

CAPTAIN KIDD'S TREASURE

Say the word "pirate," and one of the first names that comes to mind is Captain Kidd. In legend he was one of the most notorious pirates of them all, the terror of the seas from the Spanish Main to the Indian Ocean. In legend he was a swashbuckling buccaneer who looted the sea lanes of a fortune and left buried treasure worth a king's ransom. In *legend!* But legend and history do not always agree.

The historical Captain Kidd wasn't much of a pirate at all. He certainly didn't compare with the likes of Edward "Blackbeard" Teach, who truly was a bloody marauder and was well known for violence and cruelty. But circumstances would link Captain Kidd's name with "pirate," and make him the key figure in one of the greatest treasure hunts in history.

Scottish-born William Kidd never had any intention of becoming a pirate. He was a well-respected, middle-aged sea captain with a wife and children in the colony of New York, when he was approached by a group of London businessmen with an attractive proposal. In 1695 these men

1

arranged for Kidd to obtain a commission from King William III to sail as a privateer. He was to hunt down pirates and attack any ships sailing for France, England's principal enemy at the time. All expected the venture to be highly profitable.

In his ship the *Adventure Galley*, Kidd prowled the Atlantic and Indian Oceans and the Red Sea for two years. He did not catch a single pirate ship, and his crew became mutinous. They wanted to turn to piracy themselves. Kidd got into a heated quarrel with a gunner named William Moore. In a rage he called Moore a "lousy dog" and struck him on the head with a wooden bucket. Moore died from a fractured skull.

Pressured by his crew – or so he later claimed – Kidd captured four merchant ships and sold their cargoes ashore. These ships, he said, were sailing with French papers and so were legal prizes. But even if the French papers were legitimate (captains sometimes carried forged documents to ensure safe passage through unfriendly waters), Kidd broke the rules of his commission when he divided the money from the captures among his crew, instead of waiting until their return home.

Then, on January 30, 1698, Captain Kidd committed the act of piracy that would seal his doom and make his name infamous. Off the coast of India he captured a large ship called the *Quedah Merchant*. The vessel's cargo included great quantities of silk, gold, and precious stones.

This was wealth beyond the crewmen's wildest dreams. Once again, because the *Quedah Merchant* carried French papers, Kidd believed that she was a legitimate prize. Kidd was further convinced of this when a Frenchman in the ship's crew was presented to him as the captain. Days later, Kidd was shocked to learn that the *Quedah Merchant* was actually an Indian ship, and that the real captain, who had been hiding, was an Englishman. Inadvertently or not, William Kidd had committed an act of piracy.

According to his later testimony, Kidd wanted to return the ship and cargo to the rightful owners. He told the crew that trouble awaited them in

England if they did not. But his rebellious crew wouldn't hear of it. Nor did they want to share the swag with their sponsors back in England. Kidd said that they threatened to kill him, and then burned his logbook. Amazingly, the crew allowed him the full forty shares of the loot that was his due as captain. Kidd said nothing about returning that part of the prize to its rightful owners. Soon after, many of his men deserted to join the crew of a real pirate.

Exaggerated stories of Captain Kidd's exploits soon began to spread along the sea-lanes of the world. When these dramatic accounts reached England, the Admiralty declared Kidd an outlaw and put a price on his head. The governors of British colonies were instructed to have Captain Kidd arrested if he showed up in their waters.

Meanwhile, the *Adventure Galley* had become unseaworthy, so Kidd began his return home in the *Quedah Merchant*. He reached the Caribbean, where he heard the news that he was wanted for piracy. Kidd might have fled and taken his chances on the open sea. Instead, he decided that he would go back home and clear his good name. He had the French papers he had taken from the captured vessels as proof that they had been legitimate prizes. He was certain that the London financiers who had sponsored his voyage would support him.

First Captain Kidd sailed to the island of Hispaniola and landed in what is now the Dominican Republic. There he transferred his loot to the hold of a new ship, the *Antonio,* a vessel he bought for 3,000 pieces of eight. Then he sailed north to his destiny.

Captain Kidd arrived in Boston on July 2, 1699. Four days later he was arrested and clapped in irons. He was shipped back to England where he languished in prison for almost two years before finally being brought to trial. His London backers abandoned him. The French papers so vital to his defense mysteriously disappeared. The English press vilified him as the most black-hearted, bloodthirsty villain who had ever trod a deck.

When he went on trial in May of 1701, Captain Kidd faced a prosecution made up of some of the best legal talent in London. Sick and weak from his long stay in a foul dungeon, he had to conduct his own defense. He made a poor job of it. There was little doubt as to the outcome of the trial. Kidd was found guilty of the murder of his crewman and of piracy. He was hanged at London's Execution Dock on May 23, 1701. His body was then gibbeted – hung in chains and a metal harness – as a warning to others, and left to rot.

Captain Kidd's trial and execution had been a huge sensation. But a question remained. What had he done with all that treasure? Before his arrest in Boston, Kidd had sent fabulous gifts of gold, diamonds, and other gems to friends and to men in high places, whom he thought might help him with his legal troubles. After his arrest, police searched his lodgings and his ship. They also learned of a cache he had buried on Gardiner's Island at the eastern tip of Long Island, New York. The inventory of recovered booty included 1,111 ounces (31.5 kg) of gold, 2,353 ounces (67 kg) of silver, and more than a pound (.5 kg) of precious stones. Rumors circulated on both sides of the Atlantic that there was more.

The stories gained veracity when two of Kidd's former crewmen bribed their way out of prison, sailed to Pennsylvania, and dug up a cache of gold their late captain had buried. It was valued at 2,300 pounds sterling, a fortune in those days.

Many theories have arisen as to just where Captain Kidd went between the time he left Hispaniola and arrived in Boston. People have searched for his lost treasure (if, indeed, it exists at all) from the Dominican Republic to the shores of Newfoundland. Many people believe it is at the bottom of the mysterious Money Pit on Oak Island in Mahone Bay, Nova Scotia.

That famous site has both fascinated and defied treasure hunters for more than two hundred years. Several people have lost their lives trying to unlock the secret of a carefully constructed shaft that floods every time searchers try to reach the bottom. Many other treasures besides Captain Kidd's gold are alleged to have been hidden there. The stories range from Aztec gold to a lost manuscript by William Shakespeare. Most historians agree that Captain Kidd would not have had the time, the equipment, or the manpower to construct the undersea tunnels that cause the Money Pit to flood. If Oak Island hides anything at all, it isn't likely to be Captain Kidd's treasure.

X

Many places in Atlantic Canada have intrigued treasure hunters as possible sites for the captain's gold, and tales of the supernatural have grown along with the stories of hidden booty. Pirate lore says that when an outlaw captain buried his plunder, he would kill one of his own men and inter the body with the treasure chest. The pirates supposedly believed that the dead man's ghost would protect the loot until they could return. No one knows if such a thing ever really happened, or if it is just part of pirate mythology, like the ritual of forcing prisoners to walk the plank. Of course, such stories have become part of the legend of Captain Kidd's treasure. Some of the yarns may well have been passed down through generations. Others might be the lively inventions of old sailors who, with tongue firmly in cheek, told them to big city newspapermen.

In 1877 an unidentified resident of Prince Edward Island told reporters some stories that eventually appeared in the Toronto *Globe*. He said that he had seen many places on the island and in Nova Scotia and New Brunswick where treasure hunters had dug for Captain Kidd's gold, and he knew of other sites along the New England coast. Nobody, he said, had found anything. He went on to tell of some strange occurrences that he claimed were absolutely true.

In one story, a Prince Edward Island farmer known as Brother John encountered a ghost that claimed to be the guardian of Captain Kidd's treasure. The ghost said that if Brother John would perform certain acts of charity, it would tell him where the treasure was buried. Brother John considered this a good proposition, so according to the ghost's instructions he distributed money, livestock, and the fruits of his harvest to impoverished families. The ghost then told him where to dig.

Trembling with anticipation at the prospect of becoming a rich man, Brother John went to the spot in the dead of night and began to dig. He had turned over only a few spadefuls of earth when the night was suddenly rent by a storm so violent that he had to run for shelter.

The following night Brother John went back to try again. He had barely begun to dig when a skeleton appeared to him. It said that the ghost with whom Brother John had made his bargain had lied to him, and was no longer the guardian of the treasure. If Brother John wanted the gold, he would have to make a new pact with the skeleton. Brother John thought that he had been tricked by these spectres of the night. He would make no more deals. The location of the treasure remained a secret. The narrator provided no date for this story, but gave 1876 as the certain date for his next tale.

A man named John Campbell, who was said to have "the second sight," had a dream in which he saw the place where Kidd's treasure was buried. It was a lonely spot he was familiar with on the Prince Edward Island coast. Just to be sure his vision was accurate, he engaged a man skilled in the use of a divining rod to inspect the ground. The experiment indicated that there was indeed something buried at the very spot Campbell had seen in his dream.

Like Brother John, Campbell was sure that he would soon be running his fingers through a chest full of gold doubloons and pieces of eight. So certain was he of striking it rich, that he hired sixteen men to do the digging. The men toiled for a day and a night. They shored up the sides of their excavation with timbers to keep the sand from falling in. The hole was so big, said the narrator, that it could still be seen a year later.

After hours of backbreaking work, one man struck an iron chest with his shovel. He cried, "We have found it!" The storyteller's own words describe what happened next.

"And lo, with the sound of his voice came forth thunderings and lightnings, guns firing, as though ten thousand muskets were discharged at once, swords suspended above the pit by single threads and skeletons of human forms walking to and fro, fleshless and horrible. So awful were the threatenings that the stoutest hearts quailed and they fled from the horrors which surrounded them."

The narrator had heard a third tale from an elderly Prince Edward Island lighthouse keeper. The events had taken place some forty years earlier. The lightkeeper had reason to believe that Captain Kidd's treasure was buried on an island just off Shediac, New Brunswick. He went there with two friends and began to dig. Sure enough, they uncovered a chest. Once again, lightning flashed and thunder crashed. The two friends ran in terror. The lightkeeper, though, held fast to the chest. Gradually the storm subsided. When all was quiet again, the other two men returned and demanded their share of the gold. The lightkeeper was not a greedy man, and he agreed that they would divide the money into three equal portions.

Night was falling, so the men decided to camp on the island. They built a fire, then took turns keeping watch. When the lightkeeper awoke in the morning, his two companions were gone – and so was the gold. The old lightkeeper told the narrator that he never saw his double-crossing partners again. But he'd been pleased to learn that one of them had been hanged in a foreign country.

In 1892 more amazing stories about Captain Kidd's treasure appeared in the *Globe*. In one, an old man using a divining rod found the burial place of the treasure on a beach at Smuggler's Cove, near St. John, New Brunswick. He drew a pentacle in the dirt to protect himself from evil. Then he began to dig.

Suddenly, a phantom pirate ship appeared on the water. A boat was lowered over the side, and several apparitions got into it. As the ghostly craft moved across the water toward the beach, the old man could see a commanding figure standing in the bow. It wore the clothing of a seventeenth-century sea captain, and it held a sword in one hand. The old man knew at once that these were the ghosts of Captain Kidd and his crew. Not even a pentacle could protect him from such a demonic presence. He fled in terror.

The most fantastic tale of all was told by one W.G. MacFarlane of St. John. It is unique among the many treasure stories because in it "Captain Kidd" himself reveals where he hid the gold.

In a lengthy newspaper article, MacFarlane said that one day while wandering the hills near St. John, he found a cave. He was excited because there appeared to be no evidence that anyone had ever been there before. He made a torch, and went exploring.

After making his way down a long, narrow passageway, he suddenly came upon a large chamber. He was surprised to see an old table, piles of moldering blankets and fur robes, some rusted antique guns, cooking utensils, and the remains of torches. There was also an iron chest.

MacFarlane quickly opened the chest, expecting to find glittering treasure. Instead he saw a tin box with the key still in it. In the box was a yellowed parchment covered with handwriting. MacFarlane was astonished to see that it was dated August 6, 1696 and signed by Captain William Kidd! By torchlight, he began to slowly decipher the long lines of text.

At the beginning of the parchment's narrative, Kidd is about to sail home to face the authorities. He sees no logical reason that he should not win his case, because pirates with far blacker records than his have successfully obtained pardons. Yet, he has feelings of foreboding. He says that he has hidden his treasure nearby, and is leaving directions for some fortunate soul to follow, in case he does not return. Kidd then goes on to tell his own story.

He came to know the shores of the Bay of Fundy well, he says, when he was a young privateer captain fighting the French. In a sea battle against overwhelming odds, he and his crew were forced to go ashore and make a run for it. Kidd became separated from his men, but with the help of a friendly Indian he found the cave and hid. Then he discovered a subterranean stream that led to the shore. Eventually Kidd was reunited with his men. They were able to turn the tables on their French pursuers, and they sailed away in the French ship. Kidd did not forget the cave and the secret passageway.

Then Kidd describes his tragic fall into a life of crime. He explains that he set out from England as a pirate-hunter with the best of intentions.

> "And then came the crisis of my life. We were rounding the Cape of Good Hope. It was a dark, dank, dismal night, such as Satan loves. For when he walks on earth he brings with him the atmosphere of hell that betrays his presence. That night he walked abroad and I talked with him."

The devil tempted Kidd with the wealth of the eastern seas, and the privateer became a pirate. He admits that he "reaped a rich harvest." Finally, at the end of his story, Kidd tells the secret that MacFarlane and the rest of the world yearned to know.

> " . . . find it in the passage that has the outlet at Smuggler's Cove. In the cleft of the rock, just 100 yards from the mouth. At low tide the cavern is empty of water."

9

MacFarlane said he found the underground passage and followed it, only to come to a dead end. Part of the passageway had caved in. Later he searched Smuggler's Cove for the opening at the other end. Unfortunately, the cavern described on the parchment had been obliterated by "some eruption of nature." The treasure was buried forever.

Of course, the date on the parchment MacFarlane claimed to have found was wrong. In August of 1696 Captain Kidd was in New York, preparing for his cruise to the Indian Ocean. He had not yet captured the *Quedah Merchant,* and so had no treasure to hide. Moreover, MacFarlane did not say what he had done with the parchment. The document itself would have been a valuable treasure; an autobiographical account written by the very hand of the legendary Captain Kidd!

Did W. G. MacFarlane really find that parchment, make a mistake concerning the date, and then lose the document? If so, then a treasure could still lie waiting in Smuggler's Cove.

Chapter 2

THE TREASURE OF LE CHAMEAU

Tragedy was about to strike on the very doorstep of Fortress Louisbourg, the massive French bastion on the southeast coast of Cape Breton Island – *Isle Royale,* as the French called it. It was a disaster that would result in one of the greatest treasure hunts in Canadian history. On the night of August 25/26, 1725, a horrific gale, which *Commissaire Ordonnateur* De Mezy of Louisbourg called the most frightful he had known in his thirty-five years at sea, swept in upon the island and drove the inhabitants of coastal hamlets fleeing inland. Out on the heaving, storm-lashed ocean was the ship *Le Chameau,* with three hundred and sixteen people on board. Commanded by Jean de St. James, the 600-ton, 48-gun *flute* was a jewel in the French fleet. The naval vessel had been making the voyage between Rochefort, France, and Louisbourg and Quebec since 1721. Among her passengers that fateful summer night, besides recruits for the garrisons of New France, were M. de Chazel, the new intendant of Canada; M. de Louvigny, the new governor or Trois Rivières; Major Jaques L. Hermitte, the army engineer who had designed the fortifications of Louisbourg, and the son of the governor of Montreal. In the captain's safekeeping were vital dispatches from France. In *Le Chameau*'s hold were supplies and ammunition for the troops, and in her strongbox almost 290,000 *livres* in gold, silver, and copper coins for the cash-strapped settlements; in the currency of the time, somewhere between $150,000 and $200,000.

The money never reached New France. For all the shipbuilder's craft, an eighteenth-century wooden sailing vessel was a fragile bone when caught in the maw of a North Atlantic gale and hurled upon the jaws of a reef. Just what might have been in the mind of Captain St. James can never be known. One account says he was running for the safety of Louisbourg. Another says he believed he was more than three hundred miles (480 km) from land. The end came swiftly. Just off the village of Baleine, *Le Chameau* smashed into a reef, known ever since as Chameau Rock. The ship splintered like kindling and sank. Not a single soul survived.

It was ten o'clock the following morning before any of the residents of Baleine and nearby Grand Lorambec ventured down to the beach. A grim sight awaited them. The shore was littered with bodies and wreckage. Many of the dead were undressed or in nightclothes, indicating the suddenness with which the ship had gone down. Of the horses and other livestock on board, "not even a pig came ashore alive" De Mezy would report. Pulleys washed ashore were marked with the *fleur de lys*, indicating not only that this had been a French vessel, but also that it was a King's ship. The villagers sent word to the authorities in Louisbourg, a few miles away.

On August 27, De Mezy and a party of officials and soldiers went to investigate. They found the main mast and mizzen mast and parts of the starboard side. They also found the figurehead, a camel, which identified the lost ship as *Le Chameau*. One hundred and eighty bodies were retrieved and buried in a mass grave at Baleine.

Because no portion of the stern section of the ship had washed ashore, and since the rock upon which *Le Chameau* had been crushed was under only a few feet of water at low tide, it was hoped that some of her guns and cargo might be salvaged. Then there was that richly laden paychest! Some bales of rigging and other materials were recovered, and detachments of soldiers were placed along the shore to collect useable wreckage and discourage looting. Pirates still roamed the coastal waters. They were generally wise enough to keep out of the sight of the guns of Louisbourg, but the lure of a fortune in gold and silver might bolster their courage.

It was not until the following summer that experienced divers could be brought out from Quebec to search for the strongbox. With no other protection from the cold water than a layer of grease on their naked skin, and with only the oxygen they could carry down in their lungs, these men were the daredevils of their time – especially when one considers that most Europeans (including sailors) could not swim. But for all their brave efforts, these early divers could find no trace of *Le Chameau*'s treasure.

Over the following decades, between the frequent wars, numerous attempts were made to locate the lost riches. Divers searched the sea bottom around Chameau Rock as best their primitive means would allow, but found only a few cannonballs. Then, in 1927, a fisherman hauling up his anchor saw what appeared to be a chest caught on one of the anchor's flukes. The object was at the surface for but a moment, then slipped loose and disappeared again into the depths. Certain that it had to be the now-legendary treasure chest from *Le Chameau*, divers optimistically went down to find it. But no one did. It was as though the sea were teasing them, and then laughing.

In 1949, maritime author Edward Rowe Snow of New England went down in a diving outfit that allowed him to descend to forty feet (12 m). His only souvenir of that adventure was a cannonball from *Le Chameau*. He would learn a little over fifteen years later that he had been almost on top of a king's ransom in gold and silver. But in the gloom of deep water, a near miss is as good as a mile.

Then, in 1961, young Alex Storm of Holland took up the search. He had been in the fishing community of Louisbourg, Nova Scotia, for about a year. SCUBA diving was his hobby, and he was fascinated by the tales of shipwrecks and treasure with which Cape Breton abounded. He became particularly interested in the story of *Le Chameau*. On one of his dives, he actually touched cannons and cannonballs from the doomed ship. He was thrilled. Then he found a coin, believed to be the first to be brought up from *Le Chameau*. Alex Storm was determined to find the rest.

However, five other men told Storm that they had a claim on the wreck site. They held a permit issued by the Receiver of Wrecks, and they alone had the right to search for the treasure. Storm and the five men formed a partnership. But by 1962, as the Toronto *Globe and Mail* would later report, it seemed that only Storm was pushing the search (he claimed), receiving very little cooperation from his partners. Storm terminated his contract with the five, believing it was now invalid.

Storm went to work on the project to restore the old Fortress of Louisbourg, but did not give up his quest for the treasure of *Le Chameau*. He applied for a license to search for the wreck and it was granted, on the condition that he give ten percent of whatever he found to the Nova Scotia government. In 1965 he formed a new partnership with David MacEachern and Harvey MacLeod of Louisbourg and the men began diving that summer. They searched the seafloor systematically, Storm and MacEachern doing the underwater work, while MacLeod handled their boat, the *Marilyn B.II*. Their efforts were rewarded when in seventy feet (21.3 m) of water, just a short distance from Chameau Rock, they found ballast stones which could only be from *Le Chameau*.

They pressed on. Powerful currents made the work dangerous. Inquisitive seals were sometimes a nuisance. Bit by bit the men found a trail of cannonballs, cannons, and other artifacts: a gold watch, silver dining utensils, then the ship's anchors. The trio was able to establish the path along which the current had dragged the shattered vessel.

In September, with the diving season nearing its close, Storm spotted what appeared to be gray discs in some crevices in the sea floor. He collected some and took them to the surface. When they were cleaned up, they were revealed to be silver coins bearing the image of Louis XV of France and a date of 1725.

"I will never forget the strange feeling that came over me when I set eyes on the stacked concentration of slate-gray coins" the *Globe and Mail* later quoted Storm as saying. "It was mainly a feeling of relief to know we had not been chasing the proverbial wild goose."

The divers brought up silver coins by the sackful. Then they hit the jackpot! Under the layers of silver coins, its yellow sheen uncorroded by seawater, they found the golden legacy of *Le Chameau*. Storm later said that the discovery of the gold coins was a total surprise, because they had not been aware that the ship had been carrying gold. In addition to 876 gold coins and 7,619 silver coins, the team brought up a gold ring with a large Columbian emerald, a rare gold Chevalier's cross of the Order of St. Louis, and a wealth of artifacts in the form of silver tableware, sword hilts, and buckles. And still, Storm said, they did not think they got it all.

The men spent twenty days gathering the harvest of a two-hundred-and-forty-year-old calamity, quietly taking the coins and artifacts ashore for storage. They told no one of their find. Over the winter, Storm had samples from their treasure assessed by experts in New York, London, and Paris. The value of the treasure was estimated at $700,000 (in the millions in present-day currency), and would undoubtedly fetch more as collectors competed for the coins and rare pieces.

Not until April of 1966 did Storm and his partners tell the world of their find. Then a storm of a different nature broke. Within a week, Storm's former partners had an injunction brought against him and his new partners, requiring them to turn the treasure over to Cape Breton County Sheriff James MacKillop. The group claimed they had a prior and valid agreement with Storm, which they said he had violated. Storm argued that the old agreement had been terminated. The treasure was locked up in a bank in Sydney, Cape Breton, until the matter could be settled in court.

It took five years of appeals and counter-appeals before the Supreme Court of Canada awarded seventy-five percent of the treasure to Storm, MacEachern, and Macleod; and twenty-five percent to the other group.

Alex Storm's career did not end with the controversy over the treasure of *Le Chameau*. Before that matter was even decided, he had helped find the wreck of HMS *Feversham* in 1968, uncovering another treasure in rare antique coins. He went on to find more wrecks in the turbulent, history-laced waters of Cape Breton, and wrote a book, *Seaweed and Gold,* about his greatest treasure hunt, the quest for *Le Chameau.*

MAJOR STUDHOLME'S
IRON POT

In 1783, following the British defeat in the Revolutionary War, thousands of Loyalists – American colonists who had supported the British – fled to what is now New Brunswick to escape persecution. They built a large settlement that became the city of St. John. The pioneer community grew under the protection of Fort Howe, where Major Gilfred Studholme was in command of the garrison.

Born in Ireland in 1740, Major Studholme had been a military man for most of his life. He was an influential and well-respected man in the new community. During the war, he had discouraged an American invasion of the region, and chased away Yankee privateers. He had helped negotiate a peace treaty with local Natives, whom the Americans had been urging to attack the British. When the Loyalists arrived, Studholme assisted in their resettlement. Studholm Parish would one day be named in his honor.

The major was given a grant of five thousand acres (2.023 h) of land on the Kennebecassis River, where a tributary called the Millstream flows into it, about forty miles (64.3 km) from St. John. There in the howling wilderness he built a log house that he moved into after retiring from the army. The major had no wife or children, and so lived alone except for a woman he hired as a housekeeper.

Though Major Studholme had a good military record and was liked by everyone, he did not fare well in civilian life. It seemed he was often in debt. Poor health certainly didn't help matters. When the major died in 1792, only fifty-two years old, he was broke. Or was he?

The major's last request was that his mortal remains be buried not in a cemetery, but on his own land. He had chosen for his gravesite a spot on a high hill, not far from his house. He was laid to rest as he had wished, but the grave was not marked and in time the location was forgotten.

Almost seventy years later, a treasure story suddenly came to light. There had once been a French fort at the mouth of the St. John River. According to the story, the French commander had buried a fortune in gold, silver, and jewels to prevent it from falling into English hands. The French fort fell into disrepair, and in 1777 Major Studholme had been dispatched to either repair it or build a new fort. Studholme didn't like the location of the old fort, so he undertook the construction of Fort Howe. Did he, while inspecting the old structure, come across the treasure?

People began to wonder why the ailing officer had wanted to live out in the bush after retiring. Why had he wanted to be buried on a lonely hilltop? More stories began to circulate. Visitors to the major's house said that they had seen a big hardwood chest, but they had never seen it open. The housekeeper had supposedly told people that she had never even seen the key to the chest. She had tried to move the chest once, she said, but it was so heavy she couldn't budge it. Then one day she was surprised to find the chest open – and empty! That very day the housekeeper discovered that an iron cooking pot was missing from the kitchen. She did not make any connection between the two unusual events at the time. But people who heard the story some seventy years later did.

Soon the tale was spreading from farmhouse to tavern and from town to town. Major Studholme had found the French treasure, the story went, but had kept quiet about it. He'd retired to a life of isolation so that no one would know of his wealth. His poverty was but a ruse. He had put the gold, silver, and jewels into the iron cooking pot and buried it. He'd wanted to be interred near his treasure so that his ghost could watch over it. Soon fireside tales were being told of Major Studholme's ghost riding the countryside at night on a phantom horse. People had no doubt that the restless spirit was patrolling the backcountry roads to keep greedy mortals away from his hoard. But where exactly had the major buried his treasure? People searched for years, but no one found it.

In 1894, a St. John newspaper published the account of an anonymous narrator who told of a treasure-hunting expedition he claimed to have been part of. He said that it had happened more than twenty years earlier, when he was still a boy. It is a fascinating chronicle, because in addition to the treasure hunt, it tells of the superstitions that often accompanied tales of hidden riches.

The narrator said that three strangers arrived in his village of Apohaqui. They were not familiar with the area, so they hired him as a guide. Then they told him that they were going to find Major Studholme's iron pot. "I was young," the narrator said, "the night was dark, and the charm of mystery surrounded the adventure. I consented to go."

The young guide borrowed a crowbar from a neighbor's shed as his contribution to the party's treasure-hunting equipment. Then he climbed into their carriage and directed them along a route that wound through the forest, across the Kennebecassis River and the Millrun, and finally stopped at the foot of the hill on which Major Studholme was buried. After hiding the horse and carriage in a clump of trees, they climbed the hillside in the darkness. On top of the hill they stopped at a spot where one of the strangers said he had, in a dream, seen Major Studholme bury the treasure.

But serious treasure hunters do not rely on dreams and visions. They must also have scientific evidence.

For this group of nineteenth-century adventurers, that came in the form of a mineral rod. It was a three-pronged hollow rod, quite likely of willow, filled with quicksilver (mercury) and wrapped in whalebone. Not just anybody could use a mineral rod. It had to be in the hands of a person who was sensitive to its power. The only one in the party with that ability was a young blacksmith. He held two of the prongs with his palms turned up, and walked back and forth on the hilltop. If the mineral rod "detected" treasure or anything of importance in the ground, the third prong would move up or down or from side to side. A single silver coin, it was said, was enough to lead a man with a mineral rod to buried treasure.

The men were sure that the treasure was beneath Major Studholme's unmarked grave. Nobody was comfortable with the idea of encountering the long-dead officer's bones, especially in such a lonely place and in the dead of night. And what about that ghostly horseman?

To their relief, the mineral rod led them not to a grave, which they knew was somewhere on top of the hill, but partway down the hillside to a tall, scraggy pine. There the rod bent downward. As the narrator commented, "There is no arguing with a mineral rod, even on a dark and gloomy night." They would not have to dig up the major after all.

The men looked at each other. "It's there!" one of them said.

"Yes, sir! That's where it is," said another.

Before the men could start digging, there was a ritual they had to perform to protect themselves from evil and to prevent the treasure from disappearing. First the blacksmith drew a sword and traced a large circle in the earth around the treasure site. Then he placed an open bible on the ground. A third rite called for the ground to be sprinkled with the blood of a black hen, but the treasure hunters dismissed that particular measure as ridiculous.

The blacksmith advised them that when they began digging, not one grain of earth was to be tossed outside the circle he had traced. Also, they must work in absolute silence. Not a word was to be spoken, or the spirits that guarded the treasure would take it away. So with grim faces, the three silent men and the boy stepped into the circle.

Two of the men dug while the young narrator probed down into the earth with his crowbar. The blacksmith patrolled the circumference of the circle with his sword. He waved the blade in the air to ward off any spirits that might be lurking in the darkness.

As the boy worked, memories came to him of stories he'd heard about other people who had searched for Major Studholme's treasure. Some had been frightened away by the phantom horseman. One had actually been thrown out of the hole by a frightful looking apparition. He began to regret joining these treasure hunters, who were, after all, strangers to him. Then . . .

"Suddenly our iron bar struck something that emitted a hollow sound. There was a quick change of significant glances, and excitement ran high. We worked with feverish energy, and presently a flat stone was turned up to our view and nothing more. We went down several feet, and at length struck solid rock covering the whole bed of the opening, and apparently as immovable as though it were a part of the solid base of the hill itself. After vainly trying to dig around it, one of our party, in sudden disgust, ejaculated: "I don't believe it's there at all!"

The blacksmith cried out angrily that the fool had broken the spell. He picked up the mineral rod, and it pointed skyward. The spirits had moved the treasure!

Undaunted, the blacksmith began again to walk the hillside with his device. Back and forth he went, hoping that the iron pot full of treasure hadn't been moved very far. After half an hour, the prong suddenly pointed downward.

One man shouted, "We've got it again!" In his excitement he swung his pick and buried the point in the ground. Once more the blacksmith cursed. The man had started digging before they could perform the necessary ritual. Now the treasure would be moved again! Sure enough, the mineral rod pointed skyward.

With little hope that he could locate the treasure a third time, the blacksmith wearily resumed pacing the hillside. As dawn approached, the mineral rod trembled in his hands, and indicated that the treasure was beneath a huge tree. The men would have to tunnel down to it.

This time everybody waited for the circle to be drawn, and all observed the rule of silence. However, hacking through the tangle of tree roots was extremely difficult. When the boy tried to pull out an especially stubborn piece of root, it suddenly broke. He fell backwards and the root flew from his hand and landed outside the circle. For the third time, the treasure vanished. The exhausted and exasperated treasure hunters had had enough. They returned to their homes, none the richer for their night's toil.

The treasure hunt story is fanciful, of course. But there actually was a Major Studholme at Fort Howe, and it is entirely possible that earlier French inhabitants buried valuables so the British wouldn't get them. The housekeeper's story about the empty chest and the missing iron pot might be nothing but a yarnspinner's invention. However, that doesn't mean that there isn't still treasure in the ground, whether Major Studholme found it or not.

SABLE ISLAND'S TREASURE IN THE SAND

"Graveyard" is the name given to any marine location notorious for shipwrecks. Over the centuries, few places have been more feared by sailors than Sable Island, the Graveyard of the Atlantic. More than three hundred and fifty ships are known to have been wrecked there. No doubt the waters around Sable Island claimed hundreds of other vessels that failed to reach their destinations and were listed as "missing."

Sable Island has been described as a "snake of sand," lying low and deadly about one hundred miles (160 km) off the coast of Nova Scotia. It is about twenty miles (32 km) long and a mile (1.6 km) wide, and made principally of sand. Surrounding the island for miles in every direction are submerged sandbars that are even more dangerous to shipping than the island is itself. A vessel could run aground on one of these hazards, with passengers and crew far from the relative safety of the island. The ship would then be smashed to pieces by the surf, or sucked down into one of the deep gullies between the sandbars. Sometimes a few lucky survivors would make it to the island. Often the surf would wash up nothing but wreckage and bodies.

In the days of wooden ships, sea captains had little choice but to chart courses that brought them dangerously close to Sable Island. The island and its ship-killing sandbars lay right alongside both trans-Atlantic and inter-colonial shipping lanes. It was also surrounded by rich fishing grounds. There was no shortage of victims for Sable Island. Spanish galleons, French and British warships and merchantmen, and fishing boats of many nations all came to grief in the Graveyard of the Atlantic.

People called "wreckers" took advantage of these disasters. They combed the beaches of Sable Island for anything useful that washed ashore from shipwrecks. It was common for residents of coastal communities everywhere to scavenge crates of food, liquor, clothing, and other goods after a ship broke up. Even the timbers of a wrecked ship could be used for construction. (Some people, though, believed that a house built with shipwreck timbers would be haunted by the cries of drowning sailors). There were dark rumors that on Sable Island, far from the prying eyes of authorities, wreckers even murdered the survivors of shipwrecks so they could rob them.

There were also stories of great treasures buried in the sands of the island or lying just off its shores. These treasure tales told of gold and silver from the Spanish Main, a priceless diamond from the French Crown Jewels, and of course, booty hidden by pirates like Captain Kidd. Though many of the stories were just tall tales, two ships known to have been wrecked off Sable Island actually were transporting riches.

In 1737, the *Cathrine* set sail from Workington, Ireland, for Boston. On board were two hundred and two men, women, and children. Among them were two wealthy cloth merchants who were going to set up business in Boston. They carried a lot of money in "specie" (gold and silver coins).

Some passengers had taken along their "estates," meaning all of their families' valuables, such as jewelry and gold and silver plate. The *Cathrine* was said to be the richest ship that had ever sailed out of the north of Ireland.

On the night of July 17, a violent storm drove the *Cathrine* onto a sandbar about a mile off the eastern end of Sable Island. Then the wind and surf tore the vessel from the sandbar and smashed her to pieces on the shore. Ninety-eight people were killed in the shipwreck. A few of the survivors who dragged themselves ashore died later.

The morning after the disaster, the battered castaways buried the bodies that had washed ashore. Then they built a shelter. There are no trees on Sable Island, so the survivors used timbers from the wreckage and a sail that had washed up on the beach.

The *Cathrine*'s longboat had also been tossed onto the beach. It was damaged, but the crewmen found enough tools and materials to repair it. Three days after the wreck, the captain and eight of his men set out for the mainland. Two days of hard rowing took them to Canso, Nova Scotia, about one hundred miles (160 km) away. When the commander of the garrison there learned of the tragedy, he sent a sloop to pick up the rest of the survivors. The gold and silver coins and the rest of the *Cathrine*'s valuable cargo were lost in the wreck.

One ship that went down off Sable Island actually carried a prince's treasure. In September of 1799, Prince Edward Augustus, the fourth son of King George III of England, and for whom Prince Edward Island was named, went to Halifax to take command of the military forces in British North America. Before leaving England, he arranged for a ship called the *Frances* to transport to Halifax his "equipage" – all of the gold and silver plate, expensive uniforms, and ornate military equipment that befitted a royal personage. The *Frances* sailed from England in October. She never reached Halifax.

By May of 1800, it was clear to Prince Edward that something had happened to the ship. Sir John Wentworth, the Lieutenant Governor of Nova Scotia and a personal friend of the prince, suspected that the missing vessel had run into trouble at Sable Island. He sent Lieutenant Joseph Scrambler in the cutter *Trepassy* to investigate.

When Lieutenant Scrambler reached Sable Island he could find no trace of the *Frances*. Then he spotted the schooner *Dolphin* off the north shore. The ship seemed to be trying to make a run for it. Scrambler gave chase, and after several hours caught up with the *Dolphin* and boarded her.

The captain of the schooner was a man named Reynolds, from Barrington, Nova Scotia. At first it appeared that he had nothing on board but fish, seal skins, and seal oil. But a closer inspection turned up some articles that were very interesting indeed. Lieutenant Scrambler wrote in his report:

> "She had several Trunks very much damaged on board, and appeared to have been washed on shore – one trunk was directed, His Royal Highness Prince Edward No. 2. Another trunk directed, Captain Sterling of the 7th Regiment foot, both empty. – Also a trunk containing two Great Coats, the livery worn by the Servants of His Royal Highness."

The trunks obviously came from the *Frances*. Lieutenant Scrambler asked Captain Reynolds how they came to be on the *Dolphin*. Reynolds had to do some fast talking. He explained that he had left two men to spend the winter on Sable Island hunting seals. These men said that the previous December they had seen a ship, the name of which they did not know, fighting bad weather off the north shore. Then a fog rolled in. A day later there was no sign of the ship except some wreckage that had washed ashore. There were no survivors.

Captain Reynolds gave Lieutenant Scrambler some papers from the *Frances* that the men had recovered. What he didn't tell the lieutenant was that he had visited the island earlier and salvaged crates full of soldiers' caps, silk stockings, and red coats. He had taken it all back to Barrington and sold it. Word of this business eventually reached Halifax, and Reynolds was lucky to escape prosecution. Of course, Prince Edward was not at all pleased. When he happened to see Reynolds on the street one day, he told him, "Your conduct, Sir, might do very well for Americans, but it is certainly not suitable for British subjects!"

There is no record that any of the prince's more valuable equipage survived the wreck. But another story gave rise to rumors of dark deeds on Sable Island. One of the sealers, who had told Lieutenant Scrambler about the ship he'd seen in distress, later told another man that he and his companion had found the body of a woman on the beach. The dead woman, he said, had been wearing an expensive ring. The men tried to remove the ring, but because the finger was swollen after long immersion in salt water, they couldn't get the ring off. He said they had buried the corpse with the ring still on.

There had, in fact, been a woman on the *Frances* who could have owned such a ring. She was Mrs. Copeland, wife of a prominent Halifax doctor. The Copeland family had been returning from a trip to England and was unfortunate enough to have sailed on the doomed *Frances.* But something about the sealer's story did not seem right.

Would those men, who were undoubtedly poor, have buried the woman with a costly ring on her finger? It seemed far more likely that they would have cut the finger off. Then the story took an even more sinister turn. Was the woman actually dead when they found her? Could it be that she had been alive, and they had murdered her for the ring? This was the beginning of the legend of Mrs. Copeland's ghost. It is said that she appears to visitors on Sable Island, dripping seawater. She raises one hand and shows the bloody stump where her finger was hacked off. She says that she was murdered for her wedding ring and that she cannot rest until it is restored to her. Then she vanishes.

X

There are quite likely many treasures hidden in the sands and waters of Sable Island. But finding them, other than by sheer luck, would be impossible. Because Sable Island is made of sand, the actions of wind and water cause it to move. The island's topography constantly changes. Places that were once dry land are now occupied by water. The sandbars, too, are constantly shifting. A powerful storm can alter any given part of the island overnight. The timbers of wrecks that have been buried for many years are suddenly visible, while landmarks that could be seen one day are gone the next.

Many coins and other artifacts have been found on Sable Island. However, the island and the waters off its shores are off limits to treasure hunters. Sable Island has a very fragile ecology, and so is protected by the Nova Scotia government. No one is allowed to go there without official permission. Most of the people who do visit are scientists.

But perhaps one day, while a meteorologist or an oceanographer happens to be looking on, a gust of wind or a swirl of water will move aside the sand covering a long-lost object of great value. The sunlight will shine on glittering gold, and a treasure will be found; perhaps even that of Prince Edward. It could happen.

TREASURES OF NEW FRANCE

The Seven Years War (1756–1763), known in the United States as the French-Indian War, was the climax of years of conflict between France and Britain over control of North America. French and English armies, aided by their Native allies, raided each other's territories, burning and looting. At the beginning of the war, much of what had been French Acadia (Nova Scotia and New Brunswick) was already in British hands. The French were fighting to hold onto what was left, and to thwart the British plan to capture the stronghold of Quebec. Many legends lingered after the war about French treasure left in its aftermath.

One tells of a ship, whose name has been lost, that sailed from Bordeaux, France, sometime in the late 1750s. On board were chests full of gold and silver coins, the pay for French soldiers in Canada. The ship made the Atlantic crossing without encountering any British vessels. Her captain took her around the southern tip of Nova Scotia into the Bay of Fundy.

The money in his charge was evidently destined for the French fort at Restigouche.

It would have been dangerous for the French to take the ship up the Petitcodiac River, because the British had gun emplacements there that could have blown them right out of the water. They decided it would be a better idea to transfer the payroll to smaller boats, called punts, and try to slip past the British guns at night. The French put the gold and silver coins into nine large leather bags. Then after dark they silently rowed upstream.

The plan didn't work. English soldiers saw them and set off in pursuit. The Frenchmen tried to escape across rugged, heavily wooded country. The heavy bags of coins, however, slowed them down. They were at risk not only of being captured, but also of having the payroll seized by the enemy. Somewhere in the vicinity of present-day Moncton, the French soldiers paused in their flight long enough to bury the moneybags. They drew a map showing the location. According to one account, the treasure was buried at the foot of a huge pine tree on mysterious Crow's Island, a small hill rising from the marshes between Moncton and Sunny Brae. No longer burdened with the gold and silver, the French soldiers outdistanced their pursuers and made it to their own lines.

French power in Canada collapsed with the fall of Quebec City and later Montreal. Among the French prisoners of war was one of the soldiers who had hidden the bags of gold and silver. Somehow the English learned of his connection with the money, and forced him to tell what he knew. He admitted that he had helped bury the coins, but he didn't have the map, and he could not (or would not) show the English officers the exact location. The British searched the general vicinity, but found nothing.

For more than a century the treasure was forgotten. Then, in the 1870s, the New Brunswick government allegedly received what it considered reliable evidence that there really was French gold and silver hidden near Moncton. The government financed a large-scale project to find the money (or so it is said). The treasure hunters came up empty-handed.

Then, in about 1892, an elderly Quebec man identified only as Mr. Simpson arrived in Moncton. He had a map that he claimed was the very one drawn years before by those fleeing French soldiers. The soldier to whom it had been entrusted had been mortally wounded in battle. Before he died, he gave the map to a friend. For some reason that Mr. Simpson could not explain, that friend never went after the treasure. The map had eventually come into Mr. Simpson's possession.

The map showed a spring and a south-running stream. Nearby was a large rock. The treasure supposedly was buried behind that rock.

Simpson formed a company with several local men, including Charles Blakeny, to raise money for a treasure hunt. They purchased equipment and hired engineers to help them find the place shown on the map. The men found what they were certain were the right spring and stream. But there was no big rock. The area had been well cleared of rocks for use as building stone.

The engineers could not agree on the best place to dig. Using horse-drawn ploughs, the men turned over seven acres (2.8 h) of soil, looking for ground that had previously been disturbed. In places that looked promising they dug down five feet (1.5 m). After two months they still had not found any gold or silver. Mr. Simpson, who had invested his life's savings of several hundred dollars in the project, went home broke.

Many years later, Charles Blakeny was interviewed by a newspaper reporter. He said that he had no doubt that there was treasure somewhere in the Moncton area. As a boy he had seen the skeletons of French soldiers unearthed by construction workers. They were the grisly evidence that a battle had been fought there. However, he did not think that the treasure would be found. In his opinion, the burial site had been covered by the waters of Moncton's reservoir. And there it has remained, if indeed it still exists.

X

Another story concerns the great citadel of Quebec itself. With the fall of the French fortress of Louisbourg in 1758, the Marquis de Montcalm, commander of the French army in Quebec, knew that the British army would soon be outside his walls. According to legend, he had all of the inhabitants' gold, silver, and jewelry gathered up. The total value was between two and three million dollars. The treasure was sewn into pigskin bags and then locked in brass-bound coffers. Under cover of darkness, soldiers took the hoard up the St. Charles River to a place where there was a small bay and a peninsula. There they buried it.

A year later, Quebec fell to the British after the Battle of the Plains of Abraham. Montcalm was wounded in the fight and died soon after. With him went the location of the treasure. Over time people forgot about it.

Then, sometime early in the twentieth century, an unidentified resident of Quebec City made a startling discovery. This man lived in an ancient chateau that dated back to the days of New France. He was doing some repair work on the fireplace, when he found a little silver box hidden behind a brick. In the box was an old, yellow parchment with directions to a place where a searcher would find: " . . . hidden in cement, (which probably meant plaster) charred wood, silver plate, and ingot and a sheep's skull. Under it is the secret of great wealth."

The man and his son followed the directions. Sure enough, they found the things listed on the parchment: some bits of burned wood, some silver plate and a silver ingot, and a sheep's skull. It wasn't much of a treasure. But they also found a rusted old iron chest, in which there was yet another parchment. This one had a map of the St. Charles River drawn on it, and writing in French that said:

"Pass over the river St. Charles to the wood by the little bay and
peninsula. Step out 20 feet NNW. by N. toward a grove of fir
trees. Then 50 feet by the setting sun. And, 5 feet deep embedded
in cement, lies our great treasure from the citadel."

That could only be Montcalm's lost treasure! The man and his son
were jubilant. But on their first trip across the St. Charles River they found
that the area they had to search was on land owned by the Roman Catholic
Church. That meant that any treasure buried there would rightfully belong
to the Church – unless someone could remove it quietly and unseen. Father
and son went home, and returned after dark.

They had to climb a fence to get onto the property. They found the
bay and the peninsula. Then they looked for the grove of fir trees toward
which they would have to pace twenty feet. To their great disappointment,
they saw that what had once been a grove was now a forest of fir trees!
Over a period of several nights they dug holes, hoping against hope that
they might get lucky. They didn't. If Montcalm's treasure was indeed buried
there, the chances of finding it were one in a million. One more treasure of
New France had to remain in the ground.

Chapter 6

TREASURE ON LONG POINT

Just as Sable Island is called the Graveyard of the Atlantic, Long Point is called the Graveyard of Lake Erie. Long Point is a narrow peninsula that extends twenty miles (32 km) from the Ontario shore of eastern Lake Erie, reaching almost halfway to the American side. Like Sable Island, it is made chiefly of sand, and the waters around it hide deadly sandbars. Hundreds of vessels have been wrecked here since early colonial days. Even after most of the Lake Erie shore had been settled, Long Point remained a wild, isolated place. Its folklore is full of stories about murders, ghosts, wreckers (whom the local people called "black-birds") and treasure.

One Long Point treasure tale dates from the War of 1812. A British ship called the *Mohawk* was carrying the payroll – all in coins – for the troops in that part of Upper Canada. Fearing capture by a fleet of five American ships, the captain of the *Mohawk* went ashore at Long Point and buried the money chest. Shortly after, the ship sank during a gale. Only two of her crew survived. They evidently did not know exactly where the money was buried. Over the years many people searched for the lost payroll, but nobody ever found it. It must rest there still.

The best-known tale of Long Point treasure involves a thoroughly unscrupulous man named David Ramsay, and an eccentric "doctor" named John Troyer. It is a story of bigotry, murder, and the supernatural. Some aspects of it are documented historical fact. Others will no doubt remain forever in the realm of mystery.

David Ramsay was a Scottish-born sailor in the Royal Navy who participated in the captures of Louisburg and Quebec during the Seven Years War. By the time of his discharge in 1765, he was serving on a British ship that patrolled Lake Ontario. He became involved in the fur trade, and over the next few years came to know the Great Lakes very well. Though Ramsay traded with the Natives, he despised them and mistreated them. On at least one occasion, British authorities jailed Ramsay for "irregularities committed in the Upper Province."

In the fall of 1771, David Ramsay and his seventeen-year-old brother, George, set up a trading post on Kettle Creek, about sixty miles (96.5 km) north of Lake Erie. Among their trading goods was a large quantity of rum. Their main customers were Mississauga Ojibwas. Just what happened during that winter is not clear, because Ramsay and the Natives gave conflicting accounts. One thing is certain. Ramsay emerged with blood on his hands.

According to Ramsay, the Natives repeatedly threatened to kill him because he wouldn't give them all the rum they wanted. The Natives argued that the trader had been "drunk and mad" all winter. In March, while most of the band members were away hunting, Ramsay killed and scalped a warrior named Wandagan and two women. He claimed they were drunk and had attacked him with an ax.

Ramsay and George fled down the creek to Lake Erie. At Long Point a group of Mississaugas – three warriors, a woman and a baby – caught up with them. The warriors tied the white men up, but then got drunk on the brothers' supply of rum. While their captors were intoxicated, David Ramsay managed to get loose. In a rage, he killed and scalped all five Natives, including the child. He and his brother then loaded the Natives' furs into their own canoe and went to Fort Erie. When the British authorities there learned of the murders, they arrested David Ramsay and sent him to Montreal to stand trial.

Ramsay insisted that he had acted in self-defense. Sir William Johnson, the Superintendent General of Indians, did not believe him. Johnson wrote:

"Killing a Woman and Child, and then Scalping them afterwards is inexcusable, and the Circumstances of his being able to do all this, is an evident proof that he was not in the danger he represents, and that the Inds. were too much in liquor, to execute any bad purpose."

Sir William thought that Ramsay deserved to hang for his crimes. However, he knew that a white jury was not likely to convict a white man for atrocities committed against Natives. "I don't think he will Suffer, had he killed a Hundred," he wrote in disgust. As it turned out, Sir William was right.

White settlers praised David Ramsay as a hero for "defending himself against savages." The jury acquitted him. There was not enough evidence, they said, to send him to the gallows for murder.

David Ramsay went on to prosper as a trader and a landowner. Sir William Johnson placated the angry relatives of the victims with gifts, which was customary among the Native people. There were still some among the Mississaugas who wanted revenge on Ramsay, but fear of reprisals held them back. A white man could get away with murdering Natives, but if the Natives killed a white man, they would face the wrath of Redcoat soldiers and the white man's law.

Even so, Ramsay received many threats, and there must have been moments when he feared for his own scalp. According to one story, about 1790 Ramsay and two other men went to Detroit on a trading expedition. They left the post with a fortune in furs and gold. On their way down Lake Erie, they camped near Port Stanley. A band of Natives approached them looking for liquor. Ramsay refused to give them any, and when the white men pushed off in their canoe, the Natives followed. It was no secret that the Natives hated David Ramsay. His refusal to share his rum with them certainly wouldn't help matters. He began to worry about the gold.

The white men stopped somewhere on Long Point and buried their gold, which was in an iron box. According to the legend, Ramsay killed a large black dog and dumped the body in the hole to act as guardian. Unfortunately for Ramsay, he never had an opportunity to return to Long Point. He died sometime around 1810. In stories the white settlers told, David Ramsay was a hero for killing Natives. But Mohawk chief Joseph Brant called him an "unworthy rascal."

X

About the time that David Ramsay was allegedly burying his gold on Long Point, a man named John Troyer was settling his family on a homestead on the shore of Lake Erie, just to the east of the peninsula.

A Loyalist who had come to Canada after the American Revolution, Troyer was a very complex man. He was so worried about attack by Natives, he cut rifle slits in the walls of his log house. Yet, he claimed that his Christianity forbade him to carry a rifle in the local militia.

Troyer was an ardent naturalist who studied the plants and animals of the region. He had a tremendous knowledge of botany, especially of the medicinal properties of certain plants. He was so skilled at making herbal remedies that his fellow settlers called him "Doctor" Troyer. He was also an outstanding agriculturist who planted orchards of apple, peach, plum, cherry, and pear trees.

But for all his achievements as an amateur scientist, John Troyer was extremely superstitious. He had a mortal fear of witches. He believed that they had cast spells on him that turned him into an animal at night. He kept an open bear trap at the foot of his bed so witches couldn't creep up on him while he slept. He was so convinced the widow who lived near him was a witch that he would recite magic incantations to ward off evil if she so much as spoke to him.

John Troyer lived on the Lake Erie shore for more than fifty years. Naturally, he heard the stories about David Ramsay's buried gold. Troyer believed that he had "the second sight," what people today call Extra Sensory Perception (ESP). He was also reputed to be an expert diviner, a person who could find water or minerals in the ground by using a willow wand. According to one story, Troyer decided to use his supernatural talents to find Ramsay's treasure.

Troyer went out to the place on Long Point where the gold was supposedly buried. He walked back and forth with the divining rod until he thought he had located the right spot. He had heard about the dead guard dog, and knew that certain precautions must be taken before he could dig.

Troyer and his son Michael rowed out to the treasure site late one evening. Shortly before midnight, Michael began to dig. His father stood by, holding an open bible in one hand and a glowing candle in the other. These items, they believed, would protect them from evil.

At the stroke of midnight – the witching hour, as people called it then – Michael's shovel struck something in the sand. The young man was now in a hole four feet (1.2 m) deep. He stooped down and began to clear sand away with his hands. In the flickering candlelight, father and son saw the top of an iron chest. Trembling with excitement, Michael scooped away more sand until he could reach the hasp and open the lid.

The rusted hinges screeched as Michael pulled and pried. Finally, the lid was open. Then, to the two men's horror, the form of a huge, black dog began to materialize in the hole. The terror-stricken treasure hunters fled. They scrambled into their boat and raced for home as fast as Michael could row.

Perhaps the skipper of the *Mohawk* did bury an army payroll on Long Point. Maybe the murderous David Ramsay did stash gold on the peninsula. If so, the treasures are quite likely still there, somewhere beneath the shifting sands.

Chapter 7

JOHNNY GREEN AND THE TREASURE OF THE ATLANTIC

Ships of the Great Lakes were usually freighters carrying cargoes of grain, ore, timber, and manufactured goods, not treasures of silver and gold. Sometimes, though, the safe on a passenger ship might be full of passengers' valuables, or money being transferred by a company from one city to another. This was the case with the sidewheel steamer *Atlantic,* victim of one of the worst disasters ever to occur on the lakes. It was a tragedy that would have a dramatic effect on the life of an American diver named Johnny Green.

In the dark, foggy, early hours of August 19, 1852, the *Atlantic* was making her regular Lake Erie run from Buffalo to Detroit. Captain J.B. Pettey was not happy with the overcrowding on his ship. He had been obliged to take on a large number of Norwegian and German immigrants at Buffalo. There was no cabin space for them, and now there were people sleeping on the open decks and in the companionways. Ships' owners often overloaded their vessels with freight and passengers in order to squeeze every possible cent out of a voyage. The owners also drew up tight schedules that did not allow captains to slow down in bad weather.

There were more than five hundred people on the *Atlantic* that night; about two hundred over her safe capacity. Besides all those passengers, Captain Pettey had another responsibility. In the ship's safe was $36,000 in cash and gold belonging to the American Express Company. The captain had to see the money safely delivered to Detroit.

Captain Pettey was in the wheelhouse as the *Atlantic* ploughed through fog-shrouded waters south of Long Point. Because of sandbars that extended from that dangerous peninsula, the shipping lane here was very narrow. Suddenly there was a shout from the lookout at the bow: "Steamer off the port bow!"

As the night was rent by the shrill blasts of steam whistles, Captain Pettey called down to the engine room, "Full astern!" It was too late. The bow of the propeller steamer *Ogdensburg* rammed the *Atlantic* forward of the port wheel.

At first it seemed that the *Atlantic* had been dealt only a glancing blow. The ships parted. The *Ogdensburg* stopped about a mile (1.6 km) from the site of the collision so her crew could inspect the damage to their own ship. On the *Atlantic,* a fireman hurried up to the wheelhouse to tell the captain that water was pouring into the engine room. Captain Pettey gave the order to abandon ship. There probably were not enough lifeboats and life pre-servers for all on board. Even so, what should have been an orderly evacuation quickly turned to chaos.

When the Norwegian and German immigrants saw the crew lowering the lifeboats, they panicked. None of them spoke English, so they could not understand the orders shouted to them by the ship's officers. They fought to get into the lifeboats and many jumped overboard.

The captain and crew of the *Ogdensburg* heard the screams of people in the water. Groping their way through the fog, they returned to the scene.

They rescued as many as they could, but the death toll was high. No one was sure exactly how many people had been on the *Atlantic* because the immigrants were not registered passengers. As many as three hundred people drowned that terrible morning.

The *Atlantic* went down in one hundred and sixty-five feet (50.2 m) of water, four miles (6.4 km) off Long Point and seven miles (11.2 km) inside Canadian territory. The ship was not insured. Of course, the American Express Company wanted to recover its money. The man they turned to was Johnny Green.

Since the age of fifteen, Johnny Green had been fascinated by diving. He could hold his breath for a long time, and made a good living salvaging artifacts from Great Lakes shipwrecks and selling them. Johnny also participated in rescues and recovered bodies. Eventually he had become a pioneer in the science of deep water diving. That meant wearing a clumsy protective suit, a belt of lead weights, and a large copper helmet. Air was pumped down to him through a long hose. It was a dangerous profession, but Johnny was willing to go to depths other men wouldn't dare. His accomplishments in recovering money and other valuables from Great Lakes shipwrecks were the talk of every port.

The American Express Company hired Johnny and two professional salt-water divers to recover their safe. They did not tell the men until they were at the dive site that the *Atlantic* was over one hundred and sixty feet (50 m) down. Johnny's fellow divers were stunned. One hundred and sixty feet! At that depth, they said, the water pressure would crush a man to death. They refused to dive.

But not Johnny Green. He climbed into his diving suit and belted on his weights. Before Johnny put on his copper helmet, a company official whispered the location of the safe to him. "Port side, one deck down and the third window aft the wheelhouse." Then Johnny went over the side.

Very little sunlight penetrates water to the depth at which the *Atlantic* lay. Johnny descended into a world of almost total darkness. Groping around, he found that he had been lowered directly into one of the ship's huge funnels. Then his airhose burst! Johnny tugged the emergency signal and was hauled back up to his boat.

Over the next few weeks, Johnny made several dives on the wreck. Each time his equipment proved incapable of supplying him with enough air at that depth. The water pressure caused him to suffer excruciating pain in his legs. With bad weather adding to their problems, American Express officials decided to abandon the project as hopeless. The money would just have to stay on the bottom of Lake Erie.

But Johnny Green didn't know the word "quit." According to the maritime laws of the time, a wreck that remained unsalvaged for three years became public domain. That meant anyone could keep anything they could recover from it. Johnny had become obsessed with the treasure of the *Atlantic*.

For the next three years Johnny worked for a Boston salvage firm, diving on wrecks in the Caribbean. Meanwhile, he designed two improved diving suits and developed new pumps and hoses for providing air at great depths. In August, 1855, Johnny Green was ready to go after the *Atlantic's* treasure again.

Johnny and his crew went out in the salvage schooner *Yorktown*. Over the next few days he dove several times, groping his way around the wreck in search of that third window aft of the wheelhouse. He was beginning to experience pain and dizzy spells, but nothing was going to keep Johnny Green from finding that safe.

Then, on August 23, he found the window. Johnny reached through and touched the hard steel of the safe. He surfaced immediately to get a saw and an iron bar and stayed aboard the *Yorktown* long enough to eat lunch. Then he plunged back into the lake for his appointment with destiny.

In the silent, murky depths, Johnny sawed and pried loose a section of bulkhead. Then he dragged and pushed the safe out to the deck. It was not large, but working in the darkness under all that water pressure was difficult. Nonetheless, it seemed that his three-year treasure quest was over. Johnny returned to the surface to get the hooks he would need to attach to the safe's handles so it could be raised to the deck of the *Yorktown*. He had just climbed aboard the schooner and removed his helmet when disaster struck. He collapsed on the deck in blinding pain.

People in the nineteenth century knew that pressure increases with the depth of water. But they did not understand that the pressure causes chemical imbalances in the human body. A diver ascending from depths such as those Johnny Green had been working in must do so slowly in order to decompress properly. Otherwise the diver risks an attack of a decompression sickness called the bends. This condition can be crippling, or even fatal. This time, Johnny had been too deep for too long, and had resurfaced too quickly.

On the deck of the *Yorktown,* Johnny lay paralyzed and barely conscious. His crew rushed him to the little Ontario town of Port Dover. Doctors there said he had no hope of recovery. The crew took him across the lake to Buffalo, where they hoped there might be better medical aid.

For a whole month Johnny lay in the Buffalo hospital, unable to move and at times delirious. In late September, he was sent home to Boston, where he spent the next six months bedridden with paralysis. But Johnny was tough. By the summer of 1856, he could walk with the aid of crutches.

Still determined to claim the treasure he'd practically had in his hands, Johnny returned to Lake Erie in July. He fitted out a vessel for salvage. Since he was in no condition to go down to the wreck himself, he hired two professional divers. However, when they reached the dive site, the men refused to go down.

Disgusted at what he considered to be cowardice, Johnny put on a diving suit. He was sick and still partially paralyzed, but he was going after the *Atlantic*'s treasure anyway. His men lowered him to the wreck. Johnny was in such pain that he had to crawl across the sunken schooner to the place where he had left the safe the year before. When he got there, the safe was gone!

Back on the boat, Johnny suffered another attack of the bends. He was rushed again to the Buffalo hospital. Johnny survived, but for the rest of his life he endured a twisted body and partial paralysis. While he was in the hospital, Johnny heard crushing news. Another diver had recovered the *Atlantic*'s safe.

A man named Elliot P. Harrington and several of his friends had formed their own salvage company. In June, while Johnny Green was preparing his expedition, Harrington had gone to the wreck site and evidently found the marker buoy Johnny had left there. After nearly twenty dives, during which he, too, experienced pain from the water pressure, Harrington attached a line to the safe and rode with it to the surface. He and his crew were long gone by the time Johnny Green arrived.

When they opened the safe, Harrington and friends found the $36,000 in gold and cash, as well as six gold watches. But their dreams of wealth were quickly dashed. The American Express Company learned of the salvage and claimed the money. They took advantage of a legal loophole, which Harrington's group did not contest. Harrington and his partners wound up with a total of $7,000. They had to give the rest of the money back to American Express.

Most disappointed of all, naturally, was Johnny Green. He had almost lost his life in the quest for the *Atlantic*'s treasure, and he had certainly lost his health. No longer able to dive, Johnny wrote a book about his adventures underwater. It sold reasonably well for a while. But once again fate was unkind to Johnny Green. The Civil War broke out in 1861, and books about battles and soldiers pushed his publication right off the bookstore shelves. In his final years, Johnny Green was a forgotten man. No one is sure just when he died. According to legend, he passed away in a bunk on a freighter just as it passed through a fog off Long Point.

The saga of the *Atlantic,* however, was not over. For many years the location of the wreck was lost. Then, in 1984, it was rediscovered by a Canadian diver named Michael Fletcher. This was an important find, because the *Atlantic* still contained treasure of a different sort.

The wreck lay in cold, fresh water, which meant that the structure of the ship itself, as well as the contents, would be well preserved. Each of the passengers' trunks, still in the places where the stewards had stowed them, would be a time-capsule from another age. But, as with the American Express money, more than one party was interested in this historic treasure.

Shortly after Fletcher's discovery, divers from a California-based firm went down to the wreck and removed some items, which they took to the United States. This led to a lengthy legal battle over ownership of the wreck and its contents. An Ontario court finally ruled that the *Atlantic* and all of its relics and artifacts belonged to the province of Ontario. The wreck was in Ontario waters, and the original American owners had abandoned all salvage attempts soon after the ship sank. For ten years the items were stored in a Ministry of Culture warehouse in Ottawa. Since 2002, more than six hundred artifacts from the *Atlantic* have been on display in the Port Dover Harbour Museum in Port Dover, Ontario. That is a cultural treasure of far greater value than the money Johnny Green failed to recover, and for which he paid so dearly.

Chapter 8

OUTLAW LOOT
AND THE RENO GANG

In the days of the American Wild West, outlaws were the scourge of frontier society. They plundered banks, trains, and stagecoaches, and shot it out with pursuing lawmen. Often, to escape arrest, the bandits fled to places where they believed they would be safe from authorities. Often, too, they hid their loot, expecting to return for it later. One such outlaw band was the Reno gang of Indiana who may well have stashed a fortune in stolen money in Windsor, Ontario.

The Reno brothers were among the first — and the worst — of the bandit gangs to arise in the aftermath of the American Civil War. Led by Frank Reno, the gang included his brothers, John, Simeon, and William, as well as a motley collection of thieves and saddle tramps. From their head-quarters in the town of Rockford, Indiana, the Renos terrorized the countryside, robbing banks, post offices, and public treasury offices. No one was safe from these violent, brutal men. Anyone who dared to resist them risked being shot, or having their home go up in flames.

In October of 1866, the Renos became the first outlaws in American history to hold up a train, riding away with more than $13,000. Outraged railroad officials hired the Pinkerton Detective Agency to stop the rampaging gang. Allan Pinkerton, founder of the agency, took charge of the operation himself. He soon captured John Reno, who was sent to prison. But the rest of the gang remained elusive.

The list of crimes grew as the Renos continued their rampage. Then, on May 22, 1868, the outlaws pulled their biggest job yet. Frank, Simeon, and William, and gang members Mike Rogers and Charles Anderson robbed a train near Marshfield, Indiana. They shot a conductor, threw an express clerk from the still-moving train, and got away with more than $97,000 in cash and government bonds, a sum that would amount to hundreds of thousands of dollars in today's currency. Ironically, this huge success proved to be the undoing of the Reno gang.

Pinkerton detectives were soon hot on the outlaws' trail. Within a week of the hold-up they captured Simeon and William and locked them in the jail in New Albany, Indiana. Public anger over the enormity and violence of the crime reached the boiling point. Vigilante mobs seized several men known to be associated with the Renos and hanged them without benefit of trial. Fearful that they, too, might be arrested – or lynched – Frank Reno, Mike Rogers, and Charles Anderson fled to Windsor in Canada. The border city was a well-known hangout for American desperadoes on the run. They settled down there to enjoy their ill-got gains.

Pinkerton detectives soon traced the outlaws to Windsor. They informed Canadian police, who arrested the trio. Frank Reno hired a top lawyer who took advantage of every legal loophole to prevent his clients from being returned to the United States to stand trial. He even managed to have Mike Rogers released, because none of the witnesses from the train robbery could identify him as one of the bandits. The witnesses did, however, identify Reno and Anderson.

Canadian officials knew that they had notorious criminals locked in the Windsor jail. But they were careful to observe every letter of the law in the matter of extradition (returning the men to the U.S.). They were aware of the lynchings that had taken place on the other side of the border, and they wanted assurances that the prisoners would not meet the same fate. "Hang them if you must," the Canadians told the Americans, "but at least do it legally."

Meanwhile, a worried Frank Reno plotted other means of escaping the hands of justice. He tried to break out of jail, but failed. Then he attempted to bribe a Canadian judge. The magistrate scorned the offer. Finally, Reno hired a gunman to kill Allan Pinkerton. But the tough detective grappled with the would-be assassin, disarmed him, and threw him in jail.

Canadian authorities were disgusted with Reno's behavior. The Americans had assured them that the prisoners would be protected from lynch mobs, so in October of 1868 the Canadians turned Reno and Anderson over to American police. They were certain that the outlaws would get a fair trial. They were wrong.

In the dark, early hours of December 13, a band of masked men broke into the New Albany jail, where Anderson and Frank Reno had been lodged with Simeon and William. The vigilantes overpowered the sheriff and his deputy. Then they dragged the Reno brothers and Anderson from their cells and hanged them from the rafters. It was one of the most gruesome episodes of "lynch law" in American history.

The Reno gang was gone, but what had become of their great accumulation of loot – especially the $97,000 from their last train robbery? During their brief period of freedom in Canada, the bandits had spent money freely on whiskey and gambling. Frank Reno had funds to pay legal expenses and hire the best lawyer money could buy. He also had access to plenty of potential bribe money. Now the bandits were dead. But where was their hoard?

Pinkerton detectives eventually found several thousand dollars' worth of the stolen bonds floating on the black market. But the rest of the booty had vanished. It's unlikely that Mike Rogers took it, because he was soon in prison for burglary and counterfeiting.

Police and treasure hunters searched all the Renos' old haunts in Indiana, but found no trace of the money. Frank Reno likely had taken his stolen fortune to Canada, expecting to live there in comfort, safe from the reach of American law. He probably hid the loot in Windsor, and took the secret to his grave. Many people looked for the lost treasure of the Reno gang, but no one has ever found it.

X

If Southern Ontario seems an unlikely setting for a tale about bandit treasure, the wilds of British Columbia certainly fit the bill for sagas of hidden gold. British Columbia was gold-rush country in the nineteenth century. The lure of "paydirt" drew honest prospectors, as well as hardened criminals who preferred to earn their living with a gun. One such outlaw was a Kentuckian named Boone Helm.

Helm was a killer. Mothers used his name to frighten children into obedience. In the early 1860s he was wanted by authorities in California, Oregon, Utah, and Idaho for murder, robbery – and even cannibalism. But because he was deadly with both guns and knives, few men were willing to go after him.

In 1862, Helm arrived in Victoria, British Columbia. He picked up a partner, and headed for the wild country of the Cariboo Gold Rush. The two were not interested in staking a claim. Instead they ambushed and murdered three prospectors. Friends of the dead men said that the victims had been in possession of about $32,000 in gold dust and nuggets. The killers hid the gold, then fled to the United States.

No one knows what became of Helm's partner, but it would not be surprising if Helm killed him. It wouldn't be the first time Boone Helm had turned on a companion. Helm never got a chance to retrieve the hidden gold. In 1864, he and four other outlaws were seized by a vigilante mob in Virginia City, Montana, and lynched. In all likelihood his stash of gold is still buried near some lonely trail in the Cariboo country.

X

On November 12, 1884, a man waited in ambush behind some trees at a spot on the Kootenay Trail, about twenty-four miles (38.6 km) from the town of Golden, British Columbia. His quarry was Robert Baird, a Montana liquor salesman. Baird was heading home after a successful business trip to Canada. In his saddlebags he carried more than $4,500 in cash and gold, a small fortune at that time. Traveling with Baird were a young blacksmith named Manuel Drainard and a Métis guide known only as Harry.

As the three travelers urged their horses through deep snow, they saw a man step from behind a tree and aim a rifle. The air was suddenly shattered by the crack of a gunshot. The bullet pierced Baird's chest. He tumbled from his saddle and fell dead in the snow. Drainard, who was unarmed, panicked. He spun his horse around and fled for his life. A second bullet struck Harry in the hip. But he did not run. Firing his own rifle, he rode straight at the killer. The bushwhacker shot again, but was so surprised by the Métis' bold action that he missed. Harry flung himself from his saddle and tackled the outlaw, knocking the rifle from his hands. For several minutes the two men struggled in the snow. Then, weakened by loss of blood, Harry slumped to the ground, unconscious. The bandit gave the fallen man a few savage kicks to the head, and left him for dead.

When Harry awoke some time later, he was stiff, sore, weak, and amazed that he was still alive. Nearby, Baird's naked body lay frozen in the

51

snow. Harry's own horse was gone, but Baird's was still there, stripped of its saddlebags. Harry dragged himself onto the horse's back and began a painful ride to the nearest settlement, a Canadian Pacific construction camp at Kicking Horse.

Meanwhile, the fleeing Manuel Drainard had recovered his nerve. After riding several miles from the murder scene, he turned and went back. He saw Baird's body, but Harry was gone. Drainard rode as quickly as the deep snow would allow to Golden, where he informed the police of the ambush.

From the descriptions provided by Drainard and Harry, police soon knew that their suspect was a man who went by the name of Edward Kelly, better known in the vicinity as "Bulldog." He was an American vagabond with an unsavory reputation who had been drifting around the Kootenay region for about a year.

Police quickly launched a manhunt and posted a reward of $1,250. However, the killer had made a clean getaway. The only clues police found were Kelly's spent cartridges at the murder scene and his rifle, which he had dropped in the Kicking Horse River.

Kelly managed to elude Canadian police for eight months. Then a British Columbia Provincial Police constable, working undercover, located him in a small town in Minnesota. He informed the local marshal who promptly arrested the bandit.

It should have been a routine matter to extradite Kelly to Canada to stand trial for murder. But Bulldog had connections in high places. After months of political and legal maneuvering, a slick lawyer had the extradition order nullified. Bulldog Kelly was a free man.

And what of the $4,500 taken from the unfortunate Mr. Baird? Kelly evidently had not taken it with him when he fled to the United States. After he was released, he went to work as a railway brakeman in Helena, Montana. Then, one April day in 1890, he told some co-workers that he would soon be quitting his job. He said that he was going to British

Columbia, where he would come into some money. Only minutes after making this announcement, Bulldog Kelly accidentally fell between two railway cars. His legs were crushed, and he died in hospital. Fate had accomplished what the law could not.

Why would Kelly have even contemplated a return to Canada, where a murder charge still hung over him? Historians believe that he was after the loot he had buried as he fled to the United States. If so, the gold from Robert Baird's saddlebags, worth much more today than it was in 1884, might still lie hidden somewhere in the rugged Kootenay region of British Columbia.

X

Old Sam Rowlands was one gold-rush bandit who was not as clever as he thought he was. He was another American desperado who had crossed the border into British Columbia one step ahead of the law. Early in the summer of 1892, he bought a supposedly played-out claim on Scottie Creek in the Cariboo country. For several weeks he worked the claim, turning up nothing for his toil but mud.

Then on July 19, a lone, masked gunman stopped a coach near Bridge Creek Hill. In the strongbox was $15,000 in gold dust, nuggets, and bars. The highwayman told the driver to throw down the box, and then ordered him to be on his way.

Police and civilian volunteers combed the hills in search of the bandit, but found no trace of him. Then, just a few days after the robbery, Old Sam Rowlands claimed he had struck it rich. His Scottie Creek claim was suddenly producing gold. Sam deposited about $3,000 worth of nuggets in the vault of a local store for safekeeping. He said that he had struck a "mother lode."

Other prospectors rushed to Scottie Creek to get in on the new bonanza. For weeks they panned and sluiced – and found nothing. Only grizzled Sam Rowlands was finding gold. Moreover, the old man was downright hostile toward anybody who set foot on his claim, and chased trespassers away with a gun. The other prospectors thought something was fishy. They reported their suspicions to the police in Ashcroft.

The police immediately made the connection between the robbery and Sam Rowlands' sudden "strike." They sent an undercover officer to observe him. The officer was soon convinced that Sam was laundering stolen gold through his otherwise worthless claim. Experienced prospectors examined the nuggets he had put in the vault. They could tell from texture and markings that the gold had not come from Scottie Creek at all, but from various claims all over the Cariboo. Old Sam's gold had obviously been stolen from the coach's strongbox.

Sam Rowlands was arrested, tried for highway robbery, and sentenced to four years in prison. The police seized the gold he had placed in the vault, but the old bandit refused to tell them where the rest of it was. Sam escaped from prison in 1894 and hightailed it for the American border, never to be seen in British Columbia again. It is unlikely that he had a chance to stop and recover the gold. A small fortune probably still lies hidden somewhere along Scottie Creek.

X

Somewhere between the old mining town of Camp McKinney, British Columbia, and the border town of Midway, twenty miles (32.1 km) to the southeast, there is almost certainly a stash of outlaw gold worth more than half a million dollars on today's market. On August 18, 1896, at a place just three miles (4.8 km) from Camp McKinney, a lone bandit pulled one of the biggest robberies in gold rush history.

Camp McKinney's Cariboo Mine was the most productive gold mine in the region. The yellow metal would be melted into bars and then shipped by wagon to the railway station at Midway. Usually a guard of armed miners escorted the gold shipments to discourage highwaymen. But on that day, mine superintendent A.D. Keane was making the delivery alone. Behind him in the buckboard three gold bars lay wrapped in a plain canvas sack.

As he drove the team around a sharp curve in the road, Keane was confronted by a masked man wielding a Winchester rifle. Minutes later, Keane was hurrying back to Camp McKinney with an empty wagon. The masked man had vanished into the trees with the gold.

Evidence found near the robbery scene and behind a cabin, owned by an American miner named Matthew Roderick, pointed to Roderick as the culprit. The fact that Roderick was nowhere to be found confirmed the suspicion. Several weeks after the hold-up, a Pinkerton detective traced him to Seattle, Washington.

The suspected bandit did not appear to be living the lifestyle of a wealthy man. The police decided that he had probably hidden the gold, and was waiting for things to cool down before going back for it. The police kept a watch on him. They hoped that he would make his move, and lead them to the gold. They didn't have to wait long.

Scarcely two months after the hold-up, Roderick saddled his horse and rode back to British Columbia. Detectives were right behind him. They wired ahead, and soon every trail leading to Camp McKinney was being watched. One of the men on lookout duty was A.D. Keane.

On the night of October 26, as Keane waited by a dark trail, he heard a rider approach. Keane was nervous, and he called out in the darkness, "Is that you, Matt?"

The horse stopped, and the rider dismounted. Keane heard the click of a rifle being cocked. In his fright he pulled his Colt .45 and fired. Then Keane struck a match and looked at the face of the man he had just shot. It was Matthew Roderick, dead!

The dead bandit had an empty money belt around his waist. But there was nothing on him to provide so much as a clue as to the hiding place of the gold. The location of British Columbia's biggest hoard of outlaw treasure remains a secret to this day.

Chapter 9

THE LEGENDS OF LEECHTOWN

The life of a nineteenth-century gold-rush town was usually short. When word spread of a rich strike, hopeful miners would flock to the place and stake their claims. Right behind them came the merchants, saloon keepers, gamblers, and dance hall girls, eager to get their hands on the gold dust and nuggets that the miners dug out of the ground or panned from the streams. Almost overnight a community of tents and wooden buildings would spring up. For a year or two it would be a boomtown.

Then the gold would run out. The miners would leave, looking for new places where they might strike it rich. The saloons and other businesses would close down. What had briefly been a thriving community would quickly become a ghost town. Such was the history of Leechtown on Vancouver Island. But even though its moment of glory was short-lived, Leechtown remains central to two legends about lost gold.

In July 1864, a miner named Peter Leech found gold at a site on the Leech River near the town of Sooke. Soon miners were swarming over this wild corner of Vancouver Island. Within a few months Leechtown had a population of five thousand. In a little more than a year, however, the diggings were picked clean and the people went away. But was there still gold in Leechtown? For some reason a rumor began to circulate that a notorious outlaw from California had visited Leechtown while it was still a vibrant community, and had hidden a fortune in stolen gold there.

Richard Barter was born in Canada, but went to California as a boy. He grew up in the days of the California Gold Rush, and became known as Rattlesnake Dick, one of the first bandit leaders of the Old West. Some historians say he was unjustly branded an outlaw and forced into a life of crime. Whether or not that was true, Rattlesnake Dick was the terror of the California gold fields for about three years. He and his gang pulled one robbery after another. Every lawman in the state wanted to get his hands on the desperado.

In 1856, Barter's gang pulled the biggest job of their career. They ambushed a Wells Fargo mule team carrying $80,000 in gold. Rattlesnake left the booty in the charge of his chief lieutenant, George Skinner, while he went to get mules. He wanted to replace the Wells Fargo mules, whose brands made them easily identifiable. Things started to go awry when Barter was caught trying to steal mules and tossed into jail.

Unaware that his boss had been arrested, and not sure what to do when Rattlesnake didn't return, George Skinner buried half of the gold. Then, with a posse approaching, he made a run for it. He didn't get far. Skinner was killed in a shoot-out with the lawmen. The posse recovered $40,000 of stolen gold, but the secret burial place of the rest of the loot went to the grave with George Skinner.

The authorities did not connect Rattlesnake Dick with the gold heist, and he was soon out of jail. He spent the next three years pulling small-time robberies and searching for the $40,000. Whether or not he found it is still a mystery. Like his pal George Skinner, Rattlesnake Dick Barter took secrets to the grave with him. Or did he?

On July 11, 1859, Rattlesnake's luck ran out. A sheriff named J. Boggs tracked the bandit down and shot him dead in a gunfight. Although Leechtown did not even exist yet, tales about the robber's gold were already in circulation.

Sometime after Leechtown had been abandoned, a story went around that while the town was still bustling, Rattlesnake Dick had arrived and staked a claim. He then used it to launder the stolen gold, claiming the gold had come out of his claim so that it would look like he had come by his wealth legitimately. He was in town for only a short time when a U.S. marshal showed up, arrested him, and hustled him back across the border to prison. Rattlesnake became ill in jail, and it was obvious that he had not long to live. On his deathbed, so the story went, he told the warden that he had buried the gold in a knee-high boot with a frying pan on top of it. The hoard was in Leechtown, the dying outlaw said. After Rattlesnake was dead and buried, the warden went to Leechtown to search for the gold, but found nothing.

But how could any of this be, since Rattlesnake Dick Barter died with his boots on in 1859 and Leechtown didn't exist until 1864? Could the outlaw Sheriff Boggs shot have been someone else? Could a former member of Barter's gang have taken the loot to Leechtown, and been mistaken for Rattlesnake Dick? Whatever the origin of the story, more than one treasure hunter has gone to the site of the old gold-rush town in search of treasure. All have come away empty-handed.

X

Outlaw plunder isn't the only lost treasure associated with Leechtown. Somewhere in the hills near the townsite – if one man's story is to be believed – is a lost tunnel that could lead to riches even greater than Rattlesnake Dick's bootfull of gold. This is the basis for one of Canada's strangest treasure tales.

The story goes that a man named Ed Mullard was hunting with a companion in an area between old Leechtown and a place called Jordan Meadows. Mullard became separated from his friend when he set off to follow a fresh deer trail through the bush. Dusk was falling, however, and after a while he gave up the hunt to make his way back to camp.

In the growing darkness, Mullard pushed his way through chest-high brush at the foot of a huge rock bluff. He suddenly found himself descending a stairway. He struck a match, and saw that he was standing in an oblong hole that had been cut through the solid rock. Before him were seven stone steps descending to an arch.

Curious, Mullard went down the passageway and entered a rectangular room about ten feet (3 m) long, and high enough for him to stand up in. At the end of this room, another seven steps led down to a second room. There appeared to be yet another stairway at the opposite end of this room, but there was over a foot of water on the floor, and Mullard had only matches for light. He left the tunnel, and hurried back to camp to tell his partner of his discovery. As far as is known, Mullard never visited the tunnel again. But he evidently told people about it.

In the spring of 1959, a reporter from the *Victoria Colonist* named Ted Harris heard the tale of Mullard's mysterious tunnel and contacted him. Mullard agreed to take Harris to the tunnel. However, he wanted to wait until June, when the weather would be better. One month before the scheduled date of the excursion, Ed Mullard died. He had told Harris everything he could about the tunnel – except the exact location.

The editors of the newspaper thought the Leechtown Tunnel would be a great topic for a story. They studied the few clues Ed Mullard had left behind and examined aerial survey maps of the region. Finally, they chose the southwest face of Survey Mountain as the most probable location.

On a November weekend in 1960, an expedition sponsored by the *Colonist* embarked on a search for the Leechtown Tunnel. The group included museum workers, *Colonist* staff, forest service personnel, and students. They also had the use of a helicopter.

For three days these people clambered over rocks and crawled through underbrush. They found no tunnel, and finally had to give up the search because of bad weather. One of them remarked that it would take an army to find anything in that wild country.

Some people wondered if Ed Mullard had made the story up. His friends said he wasn't the sort of person to pull a hoax. Would he have told Ted Harris that he could take him to the tunnel, if the tunnel didn't exist?

Then a man named McLaren came forward and said that he had been Ed Mullard's hunting companion the day Mullard had discovered the tunnel. He claimed to have seen the entrance to the tunnel, but had been afraid to go inside. McLaren added the ingredients that turned the mystery into a treasure tale. He said that Mullard brought out some relics he had found in the tunnel – the heads of a hammer and a pick, both very old and rusted, and a small gold bar. The bar was "three inches long, one and a half inches wide, and one inch thick." (one inch = 2.5 cm). Inscribed on the top of the bar was the word *oro* (Spanish for gold). Below it was the date 1799. However, Ed Mullard's widow said she had never seen a gold bar. And McLaren could not – or would not – tell where the tunnel was located.

In 1973, Laurence A. Lazeo, author of several booklets on British Columbia treasure, wrote that Mullard had actually found two gold bars. Lazeo claimed to have seen one of them, as well as a letter written by Mullard, giving the location of the tunnel. Lazeo said that the tunnel was not at Survey Mountain, but he provided no further information.

Since then there have been reports of people finding bottles, swords, even a cannon; all of Spanish origin. No one, however, has been able to produce these items. Could the Spanish have had a gold mine on Vancouver Island? Spain did once challenge Britain's claim to the island, and even built a fort there. But the dispute was settled diplomatically. If the Spanish found gold, they left no record of it.

Some of the stories connected to the Leechtown Tunnel are clearly in the realm of fantasy. One says that Ed Mullard found strange crystals in the tunnel. Another tells of a "white light" that follows people around. A third describes the discovery of a clearing in the bush in which nothing grows. At the centre of this clearing is a stone cairn, upon which are the bones of a horse.

Today all that remains of Leechtown are the scars in the ground where miners dug for gold. If Rattlesnake Dick's loot was ever buried there, it has yet to be found. And the Leechtown Tunnel? Was it a figment of Ed Mullard's imagination? Or does it await discovery?

Chapter 10

THE LOST LEMON MINE

Like the legendary Lost Dutchman mine of the American Southwest, the Lost Lemon Mine of western Canada straddles the line between myth and reality. Hundreds have searched for it, some making a lifelong commitment to the quest; a few even losing their lives in the process. Skeptics say it does not exist at all, except in the minds of romantic dreamers. There is a treasure trove of tales and legends concerning the elusive bonanza. Some of them agree in certain aspects; many of them contradict each other on numerous points. Most of the stories place the gold mine on the eastern slopes of the Rocky Mountains, in Alberta, but a few say it is on the British Columbia side of the line. One thing everyone does agree on is that this tale is one of Canada's most enduring legends of riches found and then lost.

The most widely accepted story involves two prospectors named Blackjack and Lemon (sometimes spelled Lemmon). Though Blackjack was reputedly the man who led the gold rush into British Columbia's Cariboo

Country, no one seems to have recorded his real name. It might have been Nehemiah Smith, but Blackjack was such a common nickname among gold hunters, outlaws, and other rugged individualists, that tracking down a specific man is almost impossible. Lemon's Christian name has also been elusive. Researchers have come up with several possibilities – among them Mark, Frank, James, and Ben – but there is no way to be certain which Lemon was Blackjack's partner.

About 1870, Blackjack and Lemon set out from the Tobacco Plains region of Montana on a gold-prospecting expedition to the North Saskatchewan River, in what would one day be Alberta. They were with a party of about three dozen men, but at some point Blackjack and Lemon broke away from this group and joined a smaller band of Métis led by a man called La Nouse. This party was heading south from the North Saskatchewan, where pickings had been slim.

It made sense for prospectors to travel in the company of other armed men, because most Natives took a dim view of gold hunters. The Natives had no use for the yellow metal themselves, but they knew that the white man had a lust for it that bordered on madness. They had seen how hordes of white men in pursuit of gold would destroy everything in their path to get at it. Gold hunters dug the ground into a muddy wasteland, they fouled the rivers, and they drove away the wildlife. It would be the discovery of gold in the Black Hills of the Dakotas a few years hence that would lead to a major clash between the Sioux Nation and the United States Army; a war that would climax in the Battle of the Little Bighorn. Gold hunters, as far as the Natives were concerned, were unwanted trespassers and fair game for a musket ball or an arrow.

Nonetheless, when the Métis party with which Lemon and Blackjack were traveling decided to ride off to a whiskey post called Fort Stand Off, the partners chose to strike out on their own. They were more interested in

gold than in a good drunk, and they evidently had considerable faith in
Lady Luck.

They followed an old Indian trail into the beautiful, unspoiled High
River country, panning the streams of fast-flowing, clear, cold water as they
went. One of them showed promising "color," flecks of placer gold. The
two men worked their way up this stream, getting better and better results
with every sample of river gravel they panned. They eventually came to a
place where the ground itself was rich with placer gold, "from grassroots to
bedrock," as the legend would say.

For prospectors, placer gold was like wages. It bought food and
whiskey, a fling at the gambling tables, and the gear for the next expedition.
One rarely got fabulously rich from it. What every prospector dreamed of
finding was the Mother Lode; the ancient deposit from which the placer
gold had come. Discovery of such a bonanza could make a man wealthy for
the rest of his days.

Blackjack and Lemon felt they were near such a find. They dug two
exploratory pits. Then, while bringing their horses in from the picket line
so they could make camp, they found it, the ledge that was the source of
the placer gold. Not little flecks that flashed in the pan, but nuggets – lumps
of almost pure gold! We do not know if either of them cried "Eureka!" but
Blackjack and Lemon knew they had struck paydirt at last.

Throughout human history, gold has been a catalyst, sometimes for
good, often for evil. It can unhinge men's minds; draw out the dark being
that exists in everyone. Blackjack and Lemon worked together, hacking and
digging and collecting the glittering nuggets. Then, after darkness fell, they
quarreled. It has never been certain just why they fought. The survivor said
later that one of them wanted to stake the claim and leave, then return in
the spring, because the season was getting late. The other man wanted to
stay and work the mine and protect it from interlopers. Claim-jumping was

a common crime. That, at least, was the story. But it could be that one man simply got greedy and wanted it all.

Exhausted from the day's work and from the stress of the argument, Blackjack rolled himself up in his blanket and lay down by the fire to sleep. Perhaps Lemon's temper was still hot from the quarrel, or maybe he acted from cold-hearted avarice. He seized an ax, a tool found in any prospector's equipment, crept up on his sleeping partner, and buried it in Blackjack's skull.

Now the gold was all Lemon's. And so was the horror and guilt over what he had done. Lemon's reason left him, driven out by the sight of the murdered man on the ground and the bloody ax in his own hands. He built up the fire – a dangerous act in hostile country – picked up his rifle, and spent the remaining hours of darkness pacing back and forth in the firelight.

Lemon did not know that his brutal deed had been witnessed, nor that even now he was being watched. Two men of the Stoney tribe, Daniel and William Bendow, had been watching Blackjack and Lemon for some time. Strange white men on Native land did not usually go unnoticed for long, and they always required careful surveillance. The two Natives, keeping under cover, had observed the gold strike and had seen what had happened in the camp, including the treacherous murder. Now they could see that the killer was clearly tormented by what he had done. They haunted him even further by uttering strange, moaning noises, which the distressed Lemon may have taken for the ghost of his slain partner, or devils awaiting him in the darkness. Perhaps it was only because they thought Lemon was mad that the Natives didn't kill him on the spot. Ironically, their trickery may well have contributed to the insanity that did overcome the prospector-turned-murderer.

With the first streak of dawn, Lemon saddled his horse and galloped away from the scene of the crime, leaving behind Blackjack's mount and a packhorse. When he was gone, William and Daniel Bendow raided the abandoned camp. They helped themselves to supplies, tools, and the two horses. They did not touch the body on the ground. A murdered white man was the white man's problem. The two Natives went back to their village and told their story to Jacob Bearspaw, chief of the Stoney tribe. Chief Bearspaw knew what would happen to his country if word of the gold reached white ears. He swore the two young men to secrecy.

Meanwhile, a distraught and incoherent Lemon made it back to the settlement at Tobacco Plains. He told the men there that Natives had killed his partner. It was the only logical explanation he could give. To turn on one's partner in the lonely wilderness was considered the vilest form of treachery, and the rough men of that time and place did not generally wait for a court of law to mete out justice. The perpetrator would be hanged from the nearest stout tree.

Lemon seemed half-crazed, and the other men put this down to his harrowing experience with the Natives. They sent a well-known mountain man named John McDougall to investigate Lemon's story. McDougall found Blackjack's body and buried it. He covered the grave with stones to protect it from animals. Then he headed back to Tobacco Plains. Apparently he was unaware of the gold strike at that time.

McDougall, too, was observed by the Natives. When the mountain man was gone, Chief Bearspaw sent his men to obliterate any trace of the white men. By the time they were finished, there was no evidence of the camp, the grave, or the mining excavations. Then, it was said, Chief Bearspaw cursed the place as evil ground. No one, on pain of death, the chief decreed, was ever to tell the whites where the gold was.

Back in Tobacco Plains, Lemon's conscience would give him no peace. It was plain to all that he was bordering on insanity, if he had not already crossed the line. Lemon finally confessed his crime to a priest, Father Jean

L'Hereux (who was not really an ordained priest at all, but a well-intentioned imposter). L'Hereux evidently said nothing to anyone about Lemon's dark deed. But Lemon had brought back the gold nuggets he and Blackjack had gathered, and gold was an almost impossible secret to keep.

Word soon spread far and wide that Lemon and the unfortunate Blackjack had struck it rich up in Canada. Lemon had spent the winter alternating between madness and lucidity, but by spring he seemed to have recovered his wits enough to agree to guide an expedition back to the Mother Lode. For weeks he and his hopeful companions combed the High River country, and from time to time Lemon claimed to recognize some landmark. But he could not retrace his steps to the place where he had bashed in Blackjack's head. As the summer wore on, his companions became impatient. They accused him of deliberately misleading them, so he could sneak back sometime and get all the gold for himself. Lemon, now a pathetic shell of a man, slipped back into madness. He became so violent, the other men had to place him under guard and take him back to Tobacco Plains. Aside from a possible sighting of him in a gold camp in 1886, Lemon then disappears from the legend. The "lost" mine, however, would continue to bear his name.

A year later Father L'Hereux himself outfitted another expedition. (Whoever said a bogus priest couldn't do a little gold hunting?) He sent to Fort Benton, Montana, for John McDougall, the mountain man who had buried Blackjack. If McDougall could lead the prospectors to the grave, it would be easy for them to find the gold mine. McDougall agreed to meet L'Hereux's party at Crowsnest Lake, but on the way he stopped at a whiskey post called Fort Kipp for a little refreshment. McDougall over-indulged in the rotgut "firewater" that passed for whiskey out on the frontier, and died, probably from alcoholic poisoning. The only white man, besides Lemon, who had seen the campsite, was gone.

Of the many other adventurers who would seek the Lost Lemon Mine, one of the most persistent was Lafayette French. He was the merchant who had originally grubstaked Blackjack and Lemon when they set out on their ill-starred expedition. The first time French went looking for the gold, he was stricken with some mysterious illness and barely made it back to civilization alive. Years later he made another attempt. This time William Bendow, one of the Indians who had witnessed the murder, agreed to defy the orders of old Chief Jacob Bearspaw, and guide French to the site for a payment of twenty-five horses and twenty-five head of cattle. But the expedition had been out only two days when Bendow suddenly became very fearful and refused to go on. French and company had to turn back.

Lafayette French was no quitter, however. Or maybe he was a man obsessed. Years later, in 1912, he again prevailed upon William Bendow to lead him to the gold. Then, as they camped one night in an abandoned ranch house by the High River, Bendow died in his sleep. French turned back again, but this time the alleged curse caught up with him. He had stopped for a visit at the home of some friends when the house caught fire. French got out of the blazing building alive, but he was horribly burned and soon died from his injuries. Before he expired, he supposedly told a friend, "I know all about the Lost Lemon Mine now." But he didn't live long enough to explain what he meant by that. Did he mean he knew where it was, or that he understood that chasing after it was a fool's errand?

Many others would search for the mine, even though historians have been able to poke holes in much of the story about Blackjack and Lemon. One of the problems with a story that is part fact and part legend is that it is difficult to separate one from the other, and people will often accept fabrication as truth, simply because it has been repeated so often. The story has been revised and distorted in retellings over the generations, so that now the truth is as difficult to find as the goldmine itself.

There are numerous variations of the tale and theories of where the gold is. The High River, Crowsnest Pass, Racehorse Creek, and Dutch Creek are but a few locations that have been considered. The Natives, so the legends say, have always known where the Lost Lemon Mine is, but they aren't talking. Chief Jacob Bearspaw had been very clear about that.

SLUMACH'S GOLD

On January 16, 1891, an elderly Coquitlan Native named Slumach was hanged at New Westminster, British Columbia. Slumach had been convicted of the murder of Louis Bee, a man of mixed white and Native blood. There was no doubt that Slumach shot Bee dead near the Pitt River in southwestern British Columbia, but his reason for the crime is still a mystery. Slumach said Bee attacked him with an ax, and he shot in self-defense. Natives who witnessed the killing said there was no such attack. Slumach, they testified, shot Bee down in cold blood. Some people claimed that Slumach and Bee had long been enemies, and that it was only a matter of time before one killed the other. However, there were those who believed that Slumach killed Bee because the man had been following him in hopes of solving the old man's big secret – the location of a hidden gold mine!

Most people agreed that Slumach was a strange man, maybe even crazy. Other Native people admired his skills as a hunter and woodsman.

But they also feared him because he had a reputation for violence. When the police were looking for Slumach after Bee's death, they had a difficult time convincing Native trackers to help them. The Natives said that Louis Bee was not Slumach's first victim. They told police that over the years Slumach had killed at least five other men. Moreover, he was rumored to have taken several women to his secret mine to do his cooking and cleaning. Those women had never been seen again. When asked what had become of them, Slumach had just said, "Drowned." Of course, people whispered that he had killed all of them to protect his secret. Police could find no evidence, however, that Slumach had killed anyone else except Bee.

Nothing is known of Slumach's early life except that he was known as a dangerous man. It was said that he would disappear into the wild Pitt Lake Mountains for weeks or months at a time. This was extremely rugged country, where the timid dared not set foot. It was inhabited by grizzly bears, wolves, and wolverines. Some people even claimed that it was the home of Sasquatch, the mysterious creature the Americans call Bigfoot.

From time to time, Slumach would show up in the frontier town of New Westminster with fistfuls of gold nuggets, some of them the size of walnuts. He would go on a wild spree in the saloons, spending money like water. He would not tell anybody, white or Native, where he found the gold. He would only vaguely hint at having found a gold mine. If anyone tried to follow him when he left town, Slumach easily gave them the slip. If some gold hungry tracker did manage to trail Slumach into the forbidding Pitt Lake Mountains, the stories said, Slumach would ambush the trespasser and kill him.

These supposed murders went undetected. It was not until Slumach killed Louis Bee that he became a wanted man. And even though he was at least sixty years old by that time, catching him wasn't easy. It was cold winter weather and starvation that finally forced him to surrender. Once he'd been tried and convicted, Slumach allegedly told his son where the gold mine was. He advised the young man to go there "only when times are bad." Before he want to the gallows, Slumach put a curse on the gold mine. He said that any man who found the gold would not take it out.

The lure of gold and the good times it could buy were too much for Slumach's son. After his father had been executed, he headed straight for the secret mine. He returned with a small fortune in gold, which he soon squandered. When the money was gone, the young fool set out for the mountains again, this time in the company of a partner. The partner returned to New Westminster alone. Slumach's son was dead on some mountainside, probably with a bullet in his back. This is but one of many versions of the beginning of a long series of disasters that befell those who attempted to discover the secret of Slumach's gold. The elusive bonanza would eventually claim almost twenty-five lives.

When the partner who had disposed of Slumach's son returned to the gold mine, he did not know he was being followed by two American prospectors, one of them a man named John Jackson. Only Jackson emerged from the wilderness alive. He had a pack full of gold, but his ordeal in hauling it out of the harsh mountain country had broken him. He was a rich man with only a short time to live. As he lay on his deathbed, Jackson claimed that to the northwest of Pitt Lake he had found gold beyond his wildest dreams. He drew two maps (or wrote down directions) showing the way to the gold. He gave one to the nurse who had been attending him, and sent the other to a friend in Seattle, Washington. Both recipients sold the documents, considering money in the hand better than a wild chase through hostile country in search of a gold mine that might not even exist. Over the years the documents passed through many hands.

In 1930, a group of men from Seattle arrived in New Westminster with one of Jackson's maps. To gather information on the Pitt Lake country, they questioned every old prospector they could find. Then they struck out to search for Slumach's gold. They found nothing but disappointment.

In 1947, a Vancouver man named Cyril Walters claimed to have been in possession of one of Jackson's maps since 1922. He had been trying every year since then to find the elusive gold mine. Twenty-five years of tramping through the mountains had gained him nothing.

Then in 1959, three local farmers decided to try their hand at prospecting. If Slumach had indeed put a curse on the Pitt Lake Mountains, it certainly was in effect as far as that expedition was concerned. The men encountered fog, rockslides, electrical storms, and ten consecutive days of pouring rain. They found no gold.

At least those men returned alive. There were many who didn't. One gold hunter dropped dead from a heart attack at the age of forty-nine. A party of RCMP constables carried his body out of the bush. Others simply vanished forever in the wild and lonely mountains. A man could easily fall into a crevice, be buried by a rockslide, or be swept off a mountainside by a torrent during a sudden storm. There was always the possibility, too, of an unfortunate meeting with a grizzly bear.

For the superstitious, there was yet another danger awaiting fortune hunters in the Pitt Lake Mountains. The ghost of old Slumach himself was said to haunt the approaches to his gold mine, guarding it against interlopers. There were tales in which Native guides agreed to take white prospectors into the mountains. When they camped at night, the ghost would appear and warn the guides not to take the white men one more step. The Natives would turn back, advising the whites that they had better do the same – if they wanted to live.

In the early 1950s, a mining company did a thorough survey of the Pitt Lake region. They found no evidence of a gold mine. Skeptics of the "lost mine" legend suggested that Slumach had invented the story to cover up the real source of his gold: murder! Might it not be possible that during his long absences, the renegade had been killing and robbing prospectors at remote diggings and on lonely trails? It would have been easy enough to conceal the murders and then let people believe a yarn about a secret gold mine.

Yet, in spite of the curse, the deadly terrain and the negative survey, one adventurer might have actually found Slumach's gold mine. R.A. "Volcanic" Brown was a veteran prospector who was something of a legend himself. He had been in on the Cariboo Gold Rush and had made a big discovery of copper. He'd had all of his teeth capped with gold. Brown was a survivor who, in spite of his advancing years, would head off alone into the most rugged country. Once, while crossing a glacier, he was caught in a raging blizzard. Several of his toes were frostbitten. When gangrene set in, Brown cut the toes off with his pocketknife.

For several years Volcanic Brown would pack up his gear in the spring and trudge into the Pitt Lake Mountains. He never told anyone exactly where he was going, and he never filed a claim. But every year, before the snows came, he returned with gold.

One night, after over-indulging in rum, Brown told a few friends a story. He said that he had come across a Native woman who was very ill. Brown knew a lot about herbal medicines, and he nursed the woman back to health. She told him that she was Slumach's granddaughter. Out of gratitude, she told him the location of the gold mine. Whether or not the story was true, Volcanic Brown continued to come down from the mountains each year with gold – until the autumn of 1931.

That September the old man failed to appear. A four-man search party led by a police officer went to look for him. They spent twenty-seven grueling days hiking up mountain trails and crossing treacherous glaciers. They finally located Brown's last camp. They found his pup tent, his shotgun, cooking utensils, and a notebook. They also found a jar containing eleven ounces (312 gr) of gold that had been hammered out of a vein. Volcanic Brown himself was gone. His body has never been found. Did the old man fall into the crevice of a glacier? Or was he finally confronted by the ghost that watches over Slumach's gold?

BIBLIOGRAPHY

Barrett, Harry B., *Lore and Legends of Long Point,* Burns & MacEachern,
Toronto, 1977

Basque, Garnet, *Lost Bonanzas of Western Canada,* Sunfire Publications,
Langley, BC, 1988

Botting, Douglas, *The Pirates,* Time Life Books, Alexandria, Virginia, 1978

Boyer, Dwight, *Great Stories of the Great Lakes,* Dodd, Mead & Company,
New York, 1966

Butts, Ed and Horwood, Harold, *Bandits and Privateers: Canada in the Age of
Gunpowder,* Doubleday Canada, Toronto, 1987

Campbell, Lyall, *Sable Island Shipwrecks,* Nimbus Publishing, Halifax, 1994

Crooker, William S., *Tracking Treasure,* Nimbus Publishing, Halifax, 1998

De Villiers, Marq and Hirtle, Sheila, *A Dune Adrift: The Strange Origins and
Curious History of Sable Island,* McClelland & Stewart, Toronto, 2004

Lazeo, Laurence A., *Lost Treasure in British Columbia,* Western Heritage
Supply Ltd., Burnaby, BC, 1973

Snow, Edward Rowe, *Unsolved Mysteries of the Sea,* Dodd, Meade & Co.,
New York, 1963

Stewart, Ron, *Mystery of the Lost Lemon Mine,* Sunfire Publications, Langley,
BC, 1993

Storm, Alex, *Seaweed and Gold,* Nimbus Publishing, Halifax, 2003

Trueman, Stewart, *Ghosts, Pirates and Treasure Trove,* McClelland & Stewart,
Toronto, 1975

Wilkins, Harold T., *Treasure Hunting,* Ivor, Nicholson & Watkins, London,
1932

ACKNOWLEDGMENTS

I would like to thank the people and institutions who were of assistance to me in one way or another while I was researching and writing this book: the terrific people at Tundra Books; the Moncton Museum in New Brunswick; the Port Dover Harbour Museum; the British Columbia Provincial Archives, the Archives of Ontario, and of course the wonderful staff of the Guelph, Ontario, Public Library.